SAMARKAND AND BEYOND

By the same author

Fiction

Snake in the Grass
A Moment in Time
Journey to a High Mountain
Woman Returning
Deep is the Night
Night in Babylon
Summer at the Castle
Action of the Tiger
Memoirs of a Cross-eyed Man
Conversations with a Witch
The Affair in Arcady
A Sound of Trumpets
A Man and His Journey
You with the Roses – What are You Selling?
The Sun-Gazers

Non-Fiction

Understanding the English
General George S. Patton
The Ancient Way
Looking at Italy
The Great Sahara
Lost Worlds of Africa
Desert Pilgrimage
By the Waters of Babylon
The Search for the Etruscans
The French Foreign Legion
The Search for Lost Worlds

James Wellard

SAMARKAND AND BEYOND

A History of Desert Caravans

Constable   London

First published in Great Britain 1977
by Constable and Company Limited
10 Orange Street London WC2H 7EG
Copyright © 1977 by James Wellard

ISBN 0 09 461410 5

Set in Monotype Garamond 11pt
Printed in Great Britain by
Ebenezer Baylis and Son Limited
The Trinity Press, Worcester, and London

Contents

Illustrations

(*Those photographs which are not otherwise attributed are by the author*)

Line Drawing and Maps

(*Maps drawn by Patrick Leeson*)

Preface

I have taken the name Samarkand as the title for this study of the caravan routes of ancient and modern times, as symbolic of a vanishing world—vanishing, but as the reader will see in the following pages, not yet altogether gone. True, James Elroy Flecker's 'golden road to Samarkand' no longer exists, and the great Silk Highway from China to Rome, a highway along which Marco Polo travelled some seven centuries ago (without let or hindrance, be it noted) is abandoned and, in any case, now passes through forbidden territory.

At the same time, the camel caravans still leave Timbuctoo for the Taodeni salt mines exactly as they have done over the last thousand years, so that it is still possible to know and experience the world that was once inter-connected by the great trade routes of prehistory.

I have been fortunate to see what is undoubtedly the last of these historic caravans, particularly in the Sahara, Eurasia, and the Arabian peninsula. I here acknowledge my debt to many anonymous caravan guides and camel-drivers with whom I have marched in my wanderings about the deserts.

I would like to thank His Excellency Haj el Faki ben Kedaze, the Tuareg Governor of Ubari; Dr M. S. Ayoub, formerly Controller of Antiquities for the Fezzan; and the Mudir of el Greifa, Abdul Rassig, who guided me into the Ramla el Dawada.

I also record my thanks to the Superintendent and staff of the Reading Room of the British Museum and other libraries that I have used; to the heads of the various Departments of

Tourism and Antiquities; and to the authors of those books and journals which I have listed in the Bibliography.

I am especially grateful to my editor Prudence Fay for her excellent advice in the preparation of this book; to Helen Baz who made the Index; and to Mrs Barbara Nelson-Smith who so competently undertook the typing of the manuscript.

J. W.

1

The Caravan

The camels which are to go on the expedition are kneeling on the outskirts of the oasis, chewing the cud with that contemptuous expression of an animal who alone, say the Arabs, knows the hundredth name of Allah. I am sitting in the sand with my pack, awaiting the signal to start, while my guide carries on an interminable dialogue with the villagers. Nobody is in a hurry: we are not catching a plane. Though our departure was set for 6 o'clock this morning so as to avoid the heat of the day, it is now past 8 o'clock, and Abdul Rassig, the guide, is still giving last-minute instructions to the villagers whose headman he is.

I have been in the Sahara long enough to know how to wait without fussing and, as a matter of fact, am quite happy to watch the camels, for I find them the most fascinating, as they are the strangest, of domesticated animals. The facetious definition of this beast is that it is a horse designed by a committee, and the creature is admittedly so curiously prehistoric that it is wonderful to study. We are told that it is of American origin, along with the llamas, vicunas, and guanocos; that it emigrated from North America via the Bering Straits; and that it was once no larger than a hare. This may be so. One does not contradict the zoologists. But whatever its origin and whoever designed it, its neck appears to have been attached to its body upside down. And does it have two œsophagi? It seems to, for the large ball of lucerne now being chewed by the big white camel whose name is Laila, is seen to descend one tube, while a replacement ascends another, the two cuds passing each other about midway up, or down, the neck.

Yes, Laila's appearance is curious, but all talk about ill temper, bad breath, and loathing of the human kind is promulgated by Westerners who only know the camel from having been photographed on the back of a bored old specimen at the base of the pyramids. It is true that the pack-camel, if covered with suppurating sores, roars with pain while being loaded; and it is obvious that, for ever after, he hates the humans who subject him to such torture. But where he is treated with affection, as among the Bedouin of Arabia, he will respond like a well-beloved dog and will even leave his companions, to whom camels are inordinately attached, to come at his master's call.

Fortunately, Laila and her two workmates look well cared for as they rest on padded knees, contentedly ruminating— aware, for all one knows, that it is they alone who make possible the crossing of the Libyan sand sea to the oases I am bound for, a country of high dunes which not even the ubiquitous Land Rover can traverse. For strange though it may seem in an age when man can walk on the moon, there are still regions left in the world for which machines are impracticable, where the camel is the only means of long-distance travel, as it was 5,000 years and more ago.

And so this scene at the Libyan oasis—the camels kneeling in the sand, the villagers standing around the well endlessly talking, the clothes they wear, the fibre ropes and sacks lying about on the sand, the two live chickens tied on top of one of the packs—this whole scene represents in miniature all the caravans that have assembled for a crossing of the desert since the beginning of recorded history. The camel-trains that brought spices to the cities of Babylonia looked like this; so did the camel caravans that crossed the American deserts during the last century.[1] The preparations have always been

[1] See Chapter 12.

the same. First, the packs are sorted out and assigned according to size and the strength of each camel; next the packs are heaved over the wooden platform which straddles the hump; then the hemp cords are tied under the animal's chest; and finally, the loading completed, the camels are commanded to rise and are led to the wooden trough from which they drink slowly and delicately, until they finally raise their small snake-like heads, shake their pendulous lips, and stand immobile, as if transfixed. It is the signal to start.

My particular small caravan is to take me into a remote region of the Fezzan province in the Libyan Sahara. This region, called the Ramla el Dawada, is unique for its ten lakes enclosed within high dunes and inhabited by some 400 negroid people known as the Dawada, literally 'Worm-Eaters'. How or when these tribesmen got shut inside their sand sea is not known, though it is probable that they were driven there by invaders. What is certain is that the unusually high dunes make it difficult for them to get out and for outsiders to get in. Land Rovers cannot negotiate the sand hills, and an aeroplane which landed in the Ramla would not be able to take off again. Helicopters, of course, could reach the three small villages of the Dawada, but there is no helicopter service in this area of the Fezzan, which, in any case, is hundreds of miles from the nearest town of any size or importance. In short, none of the oasis-dwellers along the fringes of this formidable sea has any reason to visit the 'Worm-Eaters', and the people themselves have no reason, and often no means, which would encourage them to leave their villages.

And so they remain cut off from the outside world, except for twice a year when the camel-riding Tuareg find it worth-while to cross the dunes to the three villages, carrying a few essential supplies like rice, millet, sugar, and coffee, which are bartered for the Dawada products of natron (the deposit of car-bonate of soda found in the salt lakes), and the edible 'worms'.

I am on my way to explore this strange country. We are

moving at last. Abdul the guide rides the lead camel. I follow.
The camel-driver brings up the rear. There are many myths
about camel-riding, including the popular one that it induces
seasickness. It does not. What it does induce is a sense of
discomfort which becomes almost intolerable as the mono-
tonous march continues, hour after hour. One is seated some
eight feet above the ground, perched atop a gimcrack saddle
with a high pommel in front, legs crossed, and bare feet placed
on either side of the animal's neck. Without stirrups, reins or
bridle, the rider can only communicate his wishes to his mount
by pulling on a rope attached to a ring in the camel's left
nostril, or by thumping with his feet against its neck. If the
beast should bolt—and he can, and frequently does—the rider
bounces about like a pea in a pan, and woe betide him if the
saddle slips, and he flies through the air eight feet to the hard
sand. But our little caravan proceeds sedately up and down
the dunes and along the valleys, the three camels urged on by
continual cries of exhortation or rage, to which they pay
no attention at all.

In this manner, sometimes riding, sometimes walking, we
make our way towards the dunes, keeping up, as is strictly
required in the desert, a steady three miles an hour, not
stopping for anything until Abdul locates a little bush-covered
mound, where he calls the midday halt. As soon as the camels
are hobbled, he and the camel-driver say their prayers. They
stand at attention, kneel, bow, and prostrate themselves
according to the required ritual. Then Abdul's assistant runs
off a little way into the desert with one of the chickens that has
ridden atop the white camel, cuts its throat, mutters the appro-
priate benediction, and returns with the carcase which is
quickly plucked, cleaned, cut up, and placed in the cooking-pot
with some olive oil and rice. A small fire of twigs and camel-
dung has already been lit and the pot is snugly placed on the
embers. We lie back against the sandy mound and wait for
lunch.

All over the Sahara and, for that matter, wherever deserts are still being crossed by camel caravans large or small, the scene is now the same—the camels turned loose to graze, the men squatting round the fire waiting for their midday meal. The only exceptions are the long-distance salt caravans, which we shall meet later, since the distance between the wells is often too great to permit them to stop for lunch. But where, as on our expedition, the guide knows that the next well is within a few hours' march, the caravaners see no reason to hurry in the heat of the day, especially if there is a little pasture for the camels and a little shade for themselves. Our beasts have been hobbled and have already disappeared behind a dune. Now is the time to sprawl in the sand, dozing a little, waking to stir the pot. When the chicken is cooked, it is served in battered tin dishes and eaten with rusty spoons. It tastes delicious; and so do the dried dates, which Abdul pinches with long bony fingers to find me a tender sample. That sand is sprinkled on everything we eat is not important. In fact, a meal in the desert, especially when the traveller is eating as well as we are, is something of an occasion, completed by the ritual of making the tea, green tea stiff with sugar and flavoured with mint. The teamaker must pour the contents of his little teapot from a great height without spilling a drop, until it froths like spume; and he pours and pours, back and forth, until he thinks the brew is just the right consistency. Then he will make his decision by tasting it himself, and if it is right, he pours the first cup for the guest, the next for the caravan master, and so on until each man around the fire has had the regulation three cupfuls. After the tea ceremony is over, I produce a slab of chocolate and divide it between us; and a wonderful feeling of belonging overcomes us as we sit alone in this immense and silent desolation.

What is wonderful is the sensation of sharing in a way of life which, while it has hardly anything in common with modern industrial society, is nonetheless as old as civilization itself. For there is no particular difference—except of size—between the salt caravans now crossing the Sahara a thousand miles to the south of us, and the *azalai*, the great caravans made up of thousands of camels, which conducted the Queen of Sheba from southern Arabia to Jerusalem 3,000 years ago. This is, of course, because the laws governing the caravans, like those governing the old sailing ships, cannot be changed and certainly cannot be broken. When the caravan master gives his commands, everyone obeys. If they do not, even if they cannot resume the journey because of sickness or fatigue or perhaps despair (as in the case of the slaves driven across the desert), they are simply left behind. Consequently, there is never any need for threats or any sort of exhortation: the terrain enforces the laws of survival. You must keep up with the camels, which never stop until the next stage of the march is completed. And nobody argues with the guide, even when it is evident that he has lost the way. Then one trusts in Allah to return him to his senses, for without a chart or a compass or a chronometer or any mechanical aid at all, he relies on his senses exactly as a migrating bird does. If this were not so, there would have been no blind guides in the desert, and many travellers have reported travelling with sightless men who have brought them safely to their journey's end.

I have not personally known of a blind caravan guide, but take as authentic the reports of travellers who have. Two early British observers, Thomas Pellow in 1720 and J. G. Jackson in 1810, describe how blind guides found their way across the desert by *smelling* the sand, and it is certainly the case that the colour and texture of the grains tell the expert both where he is and where to go. But irrespective of their special skills, caravaners, whether old or young (for young boys often make crossings of the desert with their fathers, as Mohammed must have done as a lad), whether in Africa or the Middle East, all have something about them which sets them apart from other men. They have in common a life of

unremitting hardship and danger—not only the hardships and
dangers which the old mariners once experienced, that is,
poor food, wretched accommodation, and occasional hurri-
canes, but in addition to these, continual hunger, thirst, heat,
and cold, and the possibility of imminent death. Add to these
privations the terrible monotony of travelling at three miles an
hour for hour after hour, day after day, across an empty
landscape, and the ordeal takes the form of genuine mental
pain. The result is not what one would expect, not what
Western psychologists would predict. The caravan men do
not become robots, or machine-men; on the contrary, they
are almost invariably philosophical, patient, and uncomplaining,
prepared to while away the time not in grumbling, but in
endless reminiscences which continue far into the night
around the camp fire. But just as they themselves are bound by
the iron discipline of desert life, so they are mercilessly intole-
rant of weakness in others and have no sympathy for a stranger
who does complain or even exhibits physical weakness or a
lack of fortitude.

Abdul, as if to demonstrate his desert expertise, dismounts
from his camel and, signalling me to follow, goes running up
the side of a dune. When I arrive he shows me how he has
scooped away the sand and how water is oozing up within
the depression he has made. He wishes to demonstrate how
much water there is even in this lifeless desert, so much that
there are actually ten small lakes in the country of the Dawada,
the largest of them at a village called Mandara which we are
now approaching. In fact, after another five hours' marching
during the late afternoon of the first day, we breast the highest
of the dunes, and there at the bottom of the slope lies an oval
sheet of water, lilac and sapphire-blue in colour, cupped
within daffodil yellow sand hills, and encircled with dark-green
palm trees—perhaps one of the most beautiful sights to be
found in any desert in the world.

'Mandara,' Abdul says, with the dignified pride of any

2

caravan guide announcing that he has brought you safely to your destination; and as is the custom of caravaners on reaching an oasis, he and the camel driver straighten their turbans and adjust their robes in order to make a suitable entry into the village.

We approach slowly, without improper haste, and the headman of the village comes forward to greet us. He is an old man, with skin the colour and texture of slate, a white moustache, and a short grizzled beard, the patriarchal representative of a race or tribe of negroes whose origin and history are absolutely unknown. The ceremonial salutations now proceed according to the strict formula of the desert. Endless phrases of greeting, repeated over and over again, are exchanged, as we are led to the headman's hut where a blanket had been spread on the sandy floor. Here we sit, smiling and nodding at each other. More village dignitaries appear at the door, crouch, come inside, and sit on their haunches, while the tea, *de rigueur* on these occasions, is prepared. A miniature hen's egg is passed to me. I am expected to break it on my thumbnail and drink it raw. After the egg, I am given a dish of the celebrated 'worms', famous throughout the Fezzan as the principal food of the Dawada and considered a powerful aphrodisiac by the Libyans. These worms, or *dood*, are actually a sort of brine shrimp whose scientific name is *artemia oudneii—oudneii* referring to the English explorer Walter Oudney who first visited these lakes in 1882 and reported their existence in an entry in his diary dated Saturday 29 June.

Clapperton [Captain Hugh Clapperton, RN, Oudney's fellow explorer] was sitting on the top of a high dune, and so pleased with the view that he called out several times for me to dismount from my camel to enjoy the treat. The appearance was beautiful . . . There is something pretty in a lake surrounded with date palms; but when every other object is dreary the scene becomes doubly so.

Oudney and Clapperton, incidentally, were the first Europeans to penetrate this far down into the Sahara, and, as far as I know, no other British traveller has ever visited the country of the Dawada. For me it had been worth the effort of the caravan march which, in any case, had not gone on long enough to become a physical and mental ordeal. Now when I had finally reached this almost mythical country and stood on the edge of the 'sapphire-blue' lake, I saw that the water was actually wine-red with billions of these minute crustaceans which spend their lives swirling round and round like an enormous mass of crimson frog-spawn. Millions of them had become stranded on the salt crust at the verge of the lake. I picked one up. It resembled a small blob of red jelly and I saw that Dr Oudney's description was perfectly correct, for the creature was a minute crustacean 'with a strong slimy smell, the eyes two large spots supported on two long peduncles; the body a row of rays on each side, like the fins of fishes.'

The shrimp are caught by girls who trudge round and round the shallows of the lake, pushing their nets ahead of them and trapping the 'worms' in eight-foot muslin bags attached to a long handle which they sweep back and forth with a scything motion. Only women are allowed to fish, and only on alternate days; and no woman is allowed to go near the lake until forty-one days after childbirth, after which she has been purified with incense. Fishing is probably connected with some pagan ritual, though the Dawadans themselves are Mohammedans.

During my wanderings in the Ramla al Dawada, our little caravan visited two other villages, each situated beside a salt lake teeming with brine shrimp; other lakes were of the fresh-water variety and contained no shrimp. Others produced natron, a product exported from the region and still used to a small extent in the Fezzan for bread-making, tanning, and the maturing of tobacco. Together with the worms, which are dried into blocks in the sun, natron forms the only item of trade exported by the Dawada and the only reason for any contact with the outside world.

The mystery of these isolated people, why and how they became prisoners of the dunes, is a still obscure chapter in the history of the Sahara, and is a story which I have tried to relate elsewhere.[1] But what it also illustrates, though undoubtedly for only a short time longer, is that in remote parts of the world, the camel caravan still represents the main artery of life itself. The entire economy of the Dawada, like certain other desert communities, is dependent upon this most ancient of transport systems, so that if the caravan for some reason, economic or political, should suddenly be discontinued, whole areas of the desert and the people that inhabit them would be affected.

I saw this in its own limited, localized way on my caravan journey to the Dawada with Abdul Rassig. I was to see it on a grander, more dramatic scale when following Saharan caravans through the Air Mountains and across the formidable sand sea called the Ténéré in the Republic of the Niger. For the truly historic caravans now survive only in the Sahara, greatest of deserts: one can no longer expect to see them along the most ancient of the international camel trails, like the Incense Road which ran from the Land of Frankincense in southern Arabia, a thousand miles northwards to the terminus at Petra in Jordan; nor do yaks, two-humped Bactrian camels, donkeys, and human porters still carry precious cargoes along the old Silk Road from Loyang in China to Antioch, via Samarkand and Tashkent—though the traveller who gets away from the airports and new motor roads of the Middle East can still see, particularly in Afghanistan, small convoys of nomads who are the descendants of the caravaners of Flecker's 'golden road'. But fortunately for the historian, there is still the Sahara, where it is possible to accompany one

---

[1] See James Wellard, *Lost Worlds of Africa*. New York: Dutton, 1967, Chapters 1–3.

of the long-distance *azalai* that still survive—like the salt
caravan that travels from the mines of Taodeni in northern
Mali to Timbuctoo—and discover for himself what that
life is like. He must be prepared in that case to endure for
days on end great physical hardship and to sustain himself on
a diet of dates and millet, supplemented, if he is lucky, by
camel milk; and there will be occasions when water is a matter
of life or death. In 1805, along this Taodeni-Timbuctoo
route, the entire caravan of 2,000 men and 1,800 camels
died because the wells were dry; and conditions are not less
hazardous to-day. For the Westerner, moreover, the absence
of all the foods he is used to—fruit, green vegetables, meat,
and fats—is bound to undermine his strength, even if he
starts out on the journey as strong as an ox. Every long-
distance caravan traveller has had the experience of reaching
the final stages of exhaustion, and the accounts of the
nineteenth-century explorers all tell the same story of near-
despair as the recitals of those who have made such journeys
in our own time. Occasionally a very unusual enthusiast for
the desert finds a sort of spiritual sublimation in his sufferings.
Wilfred Thesiger, who crossed the Empty Quarter of Arabia,
was such a person, for he tells us that when he thought he
had reached the end of his endurance, he reminded himself that
this was where he wanted to be, in the Arabian sands. Yet,

Hour after hour [he writes] my camel shuffled forward,
moving, it seemed, always up a slight incline towards an
indeterminable horizon, and nowhere in all that glaring
emptiness of gravel plain and colourless sky was there
anything upon which my eyes could focus. I would notice
some dots, think that perhaps they were far-off camels, only
to realize a few strides on that they were stones beneath
our feet. I marvelled how Rai kept his direction, especially
when the sun was overhead, since camels will never walk
straight.

We rode for seven and eight and nine hours a day without stop, and it was dreary work. Conversation died with the passing hours, and boredom mounted within me like the dull ache of pain. We muffled our faces against the parching wind, screwed up our eyes against the glare which stabbed into our heads. The flies we had brought with us from Haushi clustered black upon our backs and heads. I rode along, my body swaying backwards and forwards, backwards and forwards, to the camel's stride, a ceaseless strain upon my back which from long practice I no longer felt. I watched the sun's slow progress and longed for evening.[1]

The professional caravaner, of course, has no such literary or philosophical observations to make about his job. Crossing the desert for him is neither a spiritual nor a romantic experience: it is a way of life. He knows nothing else, and is not mentally or physically attuned to any other calling. And as far as he is concerned, the physical sufferings which all who follow camels must expect are well worth it: caravaning, in short, is, and always has been, a lucrative business, especially for the owners of camels, the merchants, and the guides. Indeed, the formidable deserts of Arabia which were crossed by the spice caravans and the equally forbidding wilderness of Takla Makan on the Silk Road would never have been conquered at all had it not been financially worthwhile for men to risk their lives doing so. Hence we must be careful not to try and identify the motives of the great explorers with those of the ancient caravaners: the former were motivated by the quest for knowledge; the latter by the incentive of profit. We are obliged, therefore, to recognize that the making of the first international highways, which contributed more than anything else to the spread of civilization, was due solely to commercial considerations. The rise of ancient city-states,

[1] Wilfred Thesiger, *Arabian Sands*. London: Longmans, 1959, pp 160, 161.

and the empires that developed from them, were all made possible by those long trains of camels and men, which the romantic-minded traveller, (if he knows where to go and has the means of getting there) can still see moving along the Saharan horizons, before passing, inevitably it would seem, into the legendary history from which they emerged.

The Oasis

For those who march with a long-distance camel caravan, there is hardly any such thing as time—that is, time neatly measured in the passing of minutes, hours, days, months, years, and finally compartmentalized into 'historical' periods. In a sense, time becomes co-existent, past, present, and future merging into space, the past seen as distance already covered, the present as the ground immediately under one's feet, and the future as the dune that rises on the horizon. So, too, places have no particular significance in terms of size or importance. In any case, the professional caravaners have no idea of the whereabouts of the world's capitals: London and New York are just as remote to them as Babylon and Nineveh. What they are conscious of is the condition of the trails which link the wells, oases, and markets between which they travel. To them the road is the reality of existence; neither time nor place are 'fixed' in our sophisticated historical sense. Consequently, in their simple and uncomplicated view of the world, every community, however remote, is connected with every other, and presumably always has been.

Similarly, those who live on the caravan routes see the passing of time not as a series of events which we read about first as newspaper headlines, then as items in the record books. To this extent, their lives are timeless: there is no 'history' for them. The pattern of existence is always the same, and the pattern depends upon the arrival of the caravans, sometimes only once a year. No Western city-dweller, preoccupied with the problem of getting a seat on the 8.30

train to his office, can imagine what it is like to await the coming of a great caravan which is to appear one morning, moving out of the empty desert and thus linking an oasis with the whole outside world. For every man, woman, and child standing on a high dune at the edge of the palmery, it is a moment of intense emotion as, in the distance, perhaps ten miles away, a long column of dark objects, apparently shapeless and immobile, is visible against the dark red horizon. Suddenly the column disappears completely, as though it had never existed. Is it a mirage? No, the caravan has passed behind a sand hill, and just as suddenly reappears, a little nearer, a little more distinguishable. All through the afternoon, the long column appears and disappears in this fashion, always, however, approaching the oasis, never stopping, never changing its formation. Soon one can see the tiny figures of men walking ahead of the lead camels, then one column, then another, then a third, several hundred camels in each formation, all moving absolutely silently and relentlessly across the vast lifeless landscape, presenting one of the most wonderful, moving, and beautiful pictures in the world.

In the meantime, the children of the oasis are wild with anticipation, for this is the most exciting event in their life. Some run out into the desert to be the first to meet the caravaners, men whom they know from previous visits, men who have occasionally given them little presents, baubles brought from the bazaars of the large towns. But the most active members of the oasis are the women: it is their duty to welcome the caravaners with food, cool drinks, and, above all, smiles and words of welcome. In fact, in the old days, they say that the husbands and grown-up sons used to absent themselves from the oasis altogether when the caravan was seen approaching, leaving their women to entertain and reward in their own fashion the men who had braved the desert.

As slowly the *azalai* emerges from the distant desert,

one begins to realize what men and beasts have endured by the sight of those single camels, far in the rear of the main columns, who no longer have the strength to march at the regulation three miles an hour. One knows that other camels have been unable to get this far and are now lying with their heads twisted back and sightless eyes staring at the sky, all the way along the trail. Perhaps some of the men have also been left behind, decently interred against the side of a dune, with a small piece of cloth on a stick to mark their last resting-place.

At last the caravan is near enough for the children to welcome it, for the men of the oasis to pick out the caravan leaders, to count the number of camels, and to assess the loads which the camels are carrying. But the sun is going down, and by ancient tradition the caravan does not come right into the oasis, but suddenly stops near the outlying date palms and at once begins to make camp. Darkness falls, suddenly the stars are out, and all over the encampment the fires of the caravaners sparkle amongst the dunes. Now it is the time for the women to hurry from their huts carrying dishes of couscous, the traditional food that always welcomes the long-distance traveller. They scurry back and forth along the sandy lanes, and the night echoes with their shrill laughter. Some are persuaded by the caravaners not to return to their homes and these stay the night, though taking care to leave before daylight so as not to be seen in public. But everyone knows who they are, of course.

In the morning the size and personnel of the caravan can be assessed as preparations are made for the last stage of the journey which, according to ancient tradition, resembles a military march-past or a Roman triumph. The captains, chief guides, and wealthy merchants have donned their ceremonial robes, embroidered caps, and the heavy swords of Tuareg origin, while the camel men start the seemingly endless task of reloading the camels. This procedure is to

Westerners who have observed it the most depressing aspect of the caravan trade, for the men responsible seem to have learnt nothing about the logistics of their *métier* since the first camels were loaded perhaps 5,000 years or more ago. The loads themselves are still of unwieldy shapes with hard corners and edges bound to cause quite unnecessary pain to the camel; and the ropes which lash these loads on to the animal's sides are of a rough dry cordage pulled so tightly under the chest and belly that they end by rubbing great sores which run with pus and provide a home for maggots. It is no wonder that the loading of these unhappy beasts of burden is accompanied by a fearful uproar compounded of snarls, groans, and a continuous roaring, until the camel is bidden to get to his feet, where he stands gurgling in his throat, still hobbled, and only able to hop as far as possible from the hated piles of bags and boxes being loaded on to his workmates' backs. One begins now to understand why the camel wears the expression he is famed for.

Eventually, out of all this characteristic disorder, the caravan is formed up and the final triumphal march into the oasis begins. The captains and guides jump on to their *meharis* which rise to their feet with a single sinuous movement; and so amid the continual roaring of those camels which consider themselves overloaded (as many are, since they have to carry the cargo of their companions who have died on the passage), the convoy enters the palmery between the two lines of citizens—women in their glittering robes and headdresses, children screeching with excitement, and the local musicians beating their drums. As the master of the caravan passes, the women break into song and shuffle back and forth waving palm leaves, while between the lines of the populace, a little ahead of the relentless columns of camels, the local cavaliers on horses not much bigger than donkeys encourage their steeds to prance about on their hind legs. Every single inhabitant of the oasis is present, even the tiniest babies well swaddled and slung on their mothers' backs.

In the centre of the oasis where the municipal buildings stand around the market square, the caravan chiefs order their camels to kneel, dismount, and walk forward to greet, and be greeted by, the local dignitaries—the mayor, chief of police, schoolmaster, and principal shopkeepers. The exchanges are in the Islamic tradition of the desert, extremely formal and repetitious, and are conducted with solemnity—no smiles, no joking, no contact other than a light touching of the other man's palm. Then these grave men disappear into various houses and the caravan continues to its usual encampment, still followed by the entire population. Unloading takes place for the last time, and for the next three or four days before starting the return journey, the caravaners know the pleasure of drinking all the water they want, eating fresh vegetables from the oasis gardens, and hearing the voices of women. After the rest period the camels will once again be loaded up, this time with the produce of the palmery— dates, salt, and natron—and the columns will move off into the sand sea. The children on the high dunes will watch them go, so slowly that they seem almost to be motionless, until, suddenly, the whole caravan disappears into the desert as though it had been nothing but a mirage.

The ritual has hardly changed in a single significant detail since long-distance caravan travel began, for there is nothing to change once the decision to cross great deserts has been made, and the methods of accomplishing it have been worked out. There are only two requirements. The first is a guide who knows not just the direction to take, but, much more important, the exact location of the wells—caravans are only lost when the next well is missed or is dry when the convoy arrives. So the absolute necessity is a guide as opposed to a compass, which is of no particular use in crossing an area of high dunes.

The second requirement is the camel and a complete knowledge of its capabilities. This knowledge is so vital to the safety of the nomads that they study the needs of their animals exactly as Western engineers study the mechanics of the motor car. The Bedouins, who have observed the nature of the camel since the time of Abraham, very quickly discovered that the camel was by far the most valuable of all animals. Some could run almost as fast as horses, and these were used in war. (We see them excellently depicted on a bronze panel in the British Museum showing Arabs fleeing from the Assyrian horse and camel cavalry.) Other and heavier camels were capable of carrying loads up to 550lbs, travelling at a steady three miles an hour for hour after hour, day after day, and needing watering on the average only every three days in the summer and not at all in cool weather, provided they could eat all the fresh fodder they wanted. In addition, this invaluable animal provided milk, meat, clothing, footwear, and even some sort of housing in the form of hides hung on sticks.

Camels are crossbred from ancient strains in the manner of our thoroughbreds, half-breds, and the like. The elegant running camel known as the *mehari* is admired for his beautiful head, his large eyes, and long, dense lashes. His hump, chest, and legs are all of a certain character, easily judged by the experts. A fine male *mehari* will be kept to service some hundred females, and he will control and dominate his harem in the manner of a buck his herd of deer. He mounts the female when she kneels down for him, placing his neck and head alongside hers and wriggling himself into the coitus position. Contrary to the popular rumour, camels do not copulate back to back; but being like the cats averse to a public display, their mating is done in private. Again, like cats, they are very conventional in their habits and hate anybody who tries to change their routine. This partly explains their reputation for bad temper; but what it amounts to is

that camels are much fonder of each other than they are of
men, except in the case of those men, like certain Bedouin
of Arabia, who treat them with the love Westerners show
for horses and dogs. But unhappily for the *djemel*, or pack-
camel, the caravaners have no sympathy for *anybody's* suffering,
including their own. As a result, most camels have come to
distrust and hate men, and they are not backward in expressing
their feelings by means of an extraordinary medley of growls,
groans, and gurgles. This behaviour starts at a very early
age, for at a year old the baby camel has his right nostril
pierced and a ring inserted. At the age of two he is branded;
at three castrated—without benefit of anaesthesia. He then
begins his life of unremitting labour, working until he is
twenty-two, which is about half his life-span, and is finally
repaid for his years of service by being slaughtered for meat.
One sometimes sees a butchered camel on the outskirts
of an oasis, still in the couched or kneeling position symbolic
of the animal and his function.

This, then, is the creature which has affected history as
much as the horse: the horse was fundamentally the servant
of the warrior, the camel of the merchant. The horse contributed to the destruction of fertile regions that were peren-
nially invaded by troops of cavalry; the camel made possible
the spread of civilization across the wastelands. By the time
of the Emperor Augustus, the great trans-continental caravan
routes linking Asia, Asia Minor, Africa, and Europe had all
been established, and along these routes passed the conveyors
of all the great philosophies and religions.

It should not be assumed that, because the caravan as a
system of transport is some 4,000 years old, it is cumbersome,
inefficient, and slow. On the contrary, it remains one of
those organizations, like the Phoenician merchant navy and
the Roman army, which are among the most efficient of
men's achievements. In all three examples, speed was not
of the essence. In any case, we should not compare their

rate of travel with ours: the fact is that we often delude
ourselves about how fast we can go from A to B; and as
every town-dweller is aware, we are often unable to say
how long it will take to reach a specific destination. The
master of a caravan, on the other hand, can predict his time
of arrival quite accurately, barring 'acts of God'. Hence
certain distances were actually based on caravan times in
classical geography, the formula used then being what it is
today: an average of thirty miles a day. This rate of travel
derives from the loaded camel's steady three miles per hour,
and the caravaners' practice of marching an average of ten
hours a day. One has to use an average for the day's journey
to allow for the nature of the terrain and the distance between
wells. Naturally for the needs of modern map-making these
rough and ready measurements are inadequate, but they
were, and still are, quite adequate for desert travel. Thus
the estimate that it takes, say, three days to go from this
oasis to that is more useful than the statement that the two
places are so many miles apart.

The problem of desert travel has always been that since
a fully loaded pack-camel can, at the limit, only march those
thirty miles a day, for three, and if pushed, four days without
watering, the caravan route must be provided with wells
every hundred miles or so. Oddly enough the great deserts,
including the Sahara, have far more water resources than the
popular image of vast sand dunes suggests. In general, there
are very few regions of the desert where wells cannot be
found within the distance of the point of no return—four
days' march. The danger is not the *absence* of wells, but the
possible error of the guide in finding them. A great many
of these water-holes are situated in the midst of what appears
to be utter desolation, without any visible signs of life to
alert the traveller to their existence. And this is the great
danger, for while it is easy to find water when an oasis with
its forest of palms is sighted, it is another exercise in desert

navigation to locate what may only be a tiny trickle of water
hidden by rocks. This is even true of the fairly large and deep
lakes in which one can actually swim in the middle of the
Air Mountains of the central Sahara: the ordinary traveller
would never dream that such reservoirs of pure cold water
are hidden in the folds of a cliff.

This fundamental need to find the hidden wells is dramatically illustrated by the grim tales told by explorers, and
none is grimmer than the experience of Conrad Kilian, the
French geologist who is credited with first discovering the
oil reserves beneath the Saharan sands. In 1928 Kilian undertook a survey of the desert between the Air and the Hoggar
Mountains, the success of his journey, and, indeed his survival,
depending upon his guide finding a well after nine days'
march. Kilian was accompanied by two camel men and
five camels. After twelve days, exhausted and with only
two litres of water left, they reached the well which Kilian
had taken the precaution of having cleared out by two Tuareg
tribesmen from the neighbouring mountains. He found the
well abandoned and a note in the Tuareg language which
read:

> Greetings to the French chief. We came to the well, but
> found it too full of sand to clear out. We are short of
> water and have to leave. Good luck!

The next well was fifty miles away. The two guides, with
customary Moslem fatalism, resigned themselves to death.

Conrad Kilian, in contrast, refused to surrender. He ordered
the camel least suffering from thirst and dehydration to be
killed and the water extracted from the contents of its stomach.
They obtained in this manner nine litres of a greenish liquid,
and another six by pressing the half-digested fodder retained
in the stomach—a liquid so nauseating that they could only
drink it when boiled and mixed with tea leaves and sugar.

Only women and girls are allowed to fish in the salt lakes of the Country of the Dawada

A platter of sun-dried 'worms', (brine shrimp) a staple food of the Dawada tribe

'The Monastery' of Petra, northern terminus of the Incense Road

Himyarite inscription from the Great Dam of Marib, capital of Sheba

Then they continued their march under the blazing sun, until the camels lay down and refused to get up again. They knew that when a camel would not rise whatever blows were rained upon it, the animal had reached its end and would lie on the sand, while the vultures on nearby rocks seldom waited to begin their attack before the camel was dead. At this point, Kilian and his two companions faced another thirty miles on foot to reach the next well. But the camels must have scented a patch of mimosa a few miles away, for they got to their feet, the march continued, and the camels were able to graze for the rest of that day while the travellers rested in what shade they could under the stunted trees. They resumed their journey after the sun had gone down, drank their last pint of water at midnight, and admitted to themselves that their end was near. And suddenly the miracle happened: they had reached the little stone parapet which trapped a trickle of water oozing from underground. Men and camels drank. Conrad Kilian slept for three days.

The large, long-distance caravans, whether commercial, military, or religious could not, of course, rely on trickles of water—not where there were thousands of camels and hundreds of people to cater for. We hear, for instance, of pilgrim caravans from Damascus to Mecca consisting of 5,000 pilgrims and 30,000 camels. One can imagine how much water was needed to satisfy this column, though it did not, of course, travel in a single block.

The problem of watering large caravans led to the development of the oases, the archetype of which was the Garden of Eden. According to the Arabs, in fact, the Garden itself is located in the oasis of Al Qurnah at the confluence of the Euphrates and Tigris rivers; and the locals will show you, if you wish, the original Tree of Knowledge in whose trunk, they say, lives a serpent. Certainly for desert-travellers the idea of paradise on earth was a place of abundant sweet water; and one has only to arrive at one of the remoter oases to appreciate what triumphs of human endeavour these green places are. For when men first reached these locations they had nothing to live on except what they had brought with them, so that they were wholly dependent on their supplies being renewed until they could cultivate first their grain and vegetable gardens, and eventually their date palms. The difficulties and dangers inherent in the creation of an oasis were so great that only negro slaves could be forced to undertake them—sinking wells, digging the underground water conduits called *foggaras*, tending the gardens, and planting the date palms.

But however fertile the oases, the fear of the caravaners is always that they will not reach the intervening wells which link these small harbours of the desert. The evidence of their sufferings is seen in the number of skeletons, human and animal, strewn around the wells: men and camels have died because the water-hole was dry when the caravan arrived, or because it had been filled in by robbers waiting to attack them. The results could be catastrophic: in 1805, 200 men and 1,800 camels perished from thirst in the desert north of Timbuctoo. An even greater disaster befell a Moroccan caravan consisting of 4,000 camels and over 1,000 men, of whom only twelve camels and twenty-one men survived.

The saga began in the dunes south of the salt mines of Taodeni, when a sandstorm lasting two days buried the caravan for so long that 300 travellers and 200 camels died of suffocation. Twenty-four days later the company, now in desperate straits, reached the valley of El Hadjar, famous for its wells. The wells were completely dry, for not a drop of rain had fallen anywhere in the Sahara for a whole year. By now 400 out of the 1,000 men, and 500 out of the 4,000 camels, had died of fatigue or thirst, and most of the cargo of salt had been jettisoned along the trail. Panic now overtook the survivors as the instinct of 'every man for himself' led them to disregard the advice of the caravan master. Eventually, however, the men realized their desperate plight and agreed to dig in unison.

They cleaned out well after well over a period of five days, without striking water. All semblance of discipline now broke down, so that when the caravan master insisted that all the camels should be killed, except 300, in order that the little water found in the slain animals, together with their blood, might enable them to push on to the next well, pandemonium broke out. No man was prepared to sacrifice his own camel, and when the sheik ordered his captains to start killing camels irrespective of ownership, a furious quarrel began and soon turned into a pitched battle in which men indiscriminately killed each other and each other's camels, drinking the blood of both humans and animals. A party of some thirty men and thirty-two camels slipped away during the following night. It was the remnants of this group—twenty-one men out of over 1,000, and twelve camels out of 4,000—which finally reached Timbuctoo.

René Caillié, the first European to return from Timbuctoo and to write an account of that fabled city, knew what these men had suffered. His caravan left Timbuctoo on 4 May and arrived at Fez in Morocco on 12 August 1828—three months on the road, traversing some 1,500 miles. The convoy of 1,400 camels laden with gold, ivory, ostrich feathers, and gum arabic, included slaves for the Moroccan market. He says that the very camels groaned when they saw the endless desert confronting them at the wells of Mourat, and he discovered why when he began suffering the torments so characteristic of caravan travel. He describes his experience as follows:

> The heat was so intense and my thirst so tormenting that I found it impossible to get any sleep; my throat was on fire and my tongue clave to the roof of my mouth . . . I thought of nothing but water—rivers, streams, rivulets were the only ideas that presented themselves to my mind during this burning fever.[1]

[1] René Caillié, *Travels through Central Africa . . . in the years 1824–1828*. London: Henry Colburn and Richard Bentley, 1830, Vol 2, p 110.

To the reader seated in his armchair with a pleasant drink to hand on the table at his side, this description of thirst may sound exaggerated. In that case, the account of the American seaman, Captain James Riley, whose brig *Commerce* was wrecked on the west coast of Africa in August 1815 and who, together with his crew, was enslaved by wandering Arabs of the Great African Desert, or Zahahrah, will, perhaps, be more convincing. Captain Riley thus describes how one quenches one's thirst *in extremis*. A camel had been butchered, its meat devoured, and its blood boiled until 'it was of the consistence of a beef's liver'.

> Notwithstanding the boiled blood we had eaten was perfectly fresh, yet our thirst seemed to increase in consequence of it. As soon as daylight appeared, a boy of fourteen to sixteen years old came running up to the camel's paunch and thrusting his head into it up to his shoulders, began to drink of its contents; my master observing him and seeing that my mouth was very dry made signs for me to go and pull the boy away and drink myself; this I soon did, putting my head in like manner into the paunch; the liquid was very thick, but though its taste was exceedingly strong, yet it was not salt and allayed my thirst. [1]

Thirst, intolerable heat by day, intense cold at night, sandstorms, and the ever-present danger of ambush have been the hazards of desert travel from time immemorial. Yet nothing, not even wars, halted for long the passage of the caravans which remained the principal, and in many regions, the only links between whole areas of the globe. Along their routes flowed the same goods which have been exchanged since the dawn of civilization. Most of these ancient highways were no longer used by advanced industrial nations by the beginning

[1] Captain James Riley, *Sufferings in Africa*. New York: Clarkson N. Poller, Inc, 1965, p 92.

of this century; hence they cannot be found on our standard atlases. But they have never really been plotted by Western geographers or, for that matter, fully recognized as the main arteries of trade and communication—even in classical times, when the bulk of the world's trade was carried along them. What, then were these roads? Where did they run? And why have they received so little attention from professional historians?

3

The Roads

The Greeks classified mankind into three categories: civilized (Greek-speaking people); barbarians (their immediate non-Greek-speaking neighbours); and savages (the others). Their view was that the three groups had little, if anything, in common: whole areas of the world were thus cut off from each other by cultural as well as geographical frontiers. And even when the peoples of Northern Europe became vaguely known to them through the reports of explorers like Pytheas of Marseilles in the fourth century BC, the assumption was that such peoples were barbarians and therefore had no connection with civilized nations. Yet we can surmise that all the early Mediterranean empires depended to some extent upon British tin, transported by the Phoenicians to manufacture the bronze weapons with which they conquered their neighbours. Since the Bronze Age flourished around 2000 BC not only in Mesopotamia, but in Scandinavia, Central Europe, and as far east as China, then a network of roads must have already existed in order to link the continents for purposes of trade and the interchange of technological skills; for it is difficult to believe that a major discovery like the fusing of two base metals was simultaneously made in localities thousands of miles apart. The probability is that the knowledge and techniques were disseminated by craftsmen who travelled with the caravans along established trade routes; and to this extent all nations were inter-connected.

We know, for instance, that around the beginning of the Bronze Age there was already an established European road system. Four Amber Roads joined the Baltic with the Mediterranean. A Tin Road ran across southern Britain to Brittany, and thence across France to Marseilles. The pack animals in the case of the European trade routes were donkeys, which were in regular service on all the main international highways well before 3000 BC and have remained in service in many parts of the world ever since. These animals, sturdy and long-suffering, marched in convoys several hundred strong, loaded with ingots of tin, bales of hides or furs, and sacks of amber. Along the caravan routes they met other convoys coming from the east or the south, and where they met, road junctions, markets, and eventually towns sprang up.

We can trace the Amber Routes across Europe from their termini on the Baltic Coast to the principal amber ports on the Mediterranean and Adriatic coasts. Indeed, the trade in this fossil resin was so important that tons of it were annually transported by caravans to the workshops and pharmacies of the ancient world, where it was prized both for its ornamental and medicinal properties. And it is certain that such valuable products as amber and tin must also have been sent eastwards to the remote nations of Central Asia and perhaps as far east as the distant kingdoms of China. Thus the European Amber Routes were really part of a world network along which not only trade but religious, cultural, and scientific exchanges continually flowed back and forth.

We should not, of course, think of these highways as being paved and signposted in motor-road fashion; but they were well-marked and well-maintained nonetheless. They needed to be, first because of the physical obstacles to easy travel—the marshes, rivers, and mountain ranges which required whole stretches of road to be constructed of layers of oak logs placed alternately lengthwise and crosswise. Elsewhere 'corduroy roads' were made of alder trunks; some sections were paved; bridges were constructed of timber. Moreover, by tacit international agreement each section of the highways was policed by the kingdom or tribe it passed through; each convoy paid tribute to the local chieftain for protection; special classes of agents, guides, and couriers were employed to facilitate communications; forts, caravanserais, and rest-houses were set up at strategic places along thousands of miles of highway.

This network of trans-European caravan roads constructed for the export of tin, amber, furs, and hides dates back to prehistoric times; soon after, at the dawn of recorded history, we hear of other great international highways linking the Far East with the new civilizations of Mesopotamia and the eastern Mediterranean. The oldest of these was the Incense and Spice Road, which originated in the South Seas of the Pacific, in islands and lands whose very names were unknown to the northern consumers. Later still, another great caravan trail stretching from China to Italy, the longest and most mysterious road of all, was added to the pattern of world trade. And finally, Africa entered the picture of international communications with the inception of the Gold Road from the interior of the Dark Continent to the North African ports serving Rome— the ancient Way of the Garamantes. Europe, Asia, and Africa were now linked in a trading system which scarcely changed until the late Middle Ages, when the Americas were reached and the ebb and flow of men and goods became global.

We shall be considering in later chapters the three principal caravan routes of antiquity, namely, the Incense Road which linked the Mediterranean with India and south-west Asia by way of Arabia; the Silk Road which joined China with the West; and the Gold Road which connected central Africa with the Mediterranean. Though these names were not current, of course, in the days when the caravans were actually using the trails, the incense, silk, and gold were cargoes whose value in the Mediterranean markets made the construction and mainten-ance of these highways possible.

How was this international trade organized? It is surprising to see how little business methods have changed in the 5,000 years that written records take us back. The system was much the same as it is today: the function of producer, merchant, middleman, carrier, and purchaser being generally what it is now. One difference was that bartered goods were often preferred to specie; but in as much as the value of the goods offered for exchange was calculated on a basis acceptable to both parties, this system was as efficient as, and of course much less complicated than, the modern system of clearing banks. We know how the barter procedure worked, for several historians have left us an account of the business, which was known as 'the Silent Trade'. The procedure involved the mutual trust of buyer and seller, since neither could understand a word of the other's language: the business was done in silence, and sometimes as in the case of the African gold trade, without the merchants even setting eyes on the gold mines. What happened was that the merchants, on arriving at the trading-post, set out the wares which they proposed to barter, then retired to their tents to await the response of the natives. We are told that the African miners laid out their gold in little piles alongside the article they wished to purchase and that if the amount was considered satisfactory, the merchants took the gold and left the proffered article behind. In the case of silk, the Silent Trade required the agents of the Western merchants to pay either in gold or in certain luxury articles manufactured in the studios and workshops of Greece and Alexandria. So gold or ready-made goods were exhibited on the floor of the frontier trading-post, and agents of the Chinese merchants made their selection in return for the proffered silk.

The caravans now started back on their long journey across deserts and mountains, to peoples and cities the producers of gold, silk, or spices had never heard of. Indeed, this international trade went on almost secretly and certainly independently of local governments and their perennial wars. One can compare it in this respect with the business in oil today: oil seems to be above politics, whether national or international. So with trade and trade routes in the heyday of the caravans: the goods had to get through. And in order to ensure the safety of these precious cargoes, the carriers were organized into specialist squads—tribesmen who knew not only the country, but the best animals for the job. Thus a bale of silk starting from Loyang in China and consigned to Rome would be carried by horses, asses, mules, two-humped camels, bullocks, human porters, dromedaries, ox carts, and sailing vessels. The entire length of the route was marked by fortresses, caravanserais, wells, markets, and custom posts. So efficient had the highway become by the first century AD, that 1,100 years later the Italian merchants, the Polos, were able to travel without let or hindrance from Constantinople to Peking via the Silk Road—a journey which would not be permitted today, even though much of the old track survives and can be traced by the ruins of towers and half-abandoned cities along its entire length.

Though international travel by the time of Augustus Caesar had become relatively safe and well-organized, very few citizens of the classical world travelled for any reason other than business. Soldiers and government officials moved about in considerable numbers, but only within the limits of the Roman *imperium*. Beyond the frontiers of civilization, travel was pretty much limited to the routes of the commercial caravans. In fact, there was no other way of travelling in safety in such regions as central Asia, the Middle East, and Africa; and all the great Victorian explorers of these areas accompanied caravans on their expeditions. Consequently we have many detailed and evocative descriptions of the great convoys of men and animals—the commercial caravans, the religious caravans bound for Mecca, and the military caravans of the sultans and beys.

[4]

The Incense Road

The oldest international caravan route in the world is the Incense Road which linked all the capitals of the ancient empires with South Arabia. The road was so heavily travelled that its very rocks have been worn smooth by the feet of tens of thousands of camels and the men who marched with them. Yet today it is almost totally forgotten, and only short sections are used by local caravans. In stretches between main cities like Mecca and Medina, the old track has disappeared altogether beneath a concrete motor-road.

The original Incense Road came into use at least 5,000 years ago, in order to meet the demand for the product of the Arabian tree, *Boswellia carteri*. The resin of this tree when burnt produces the incense which has risen from the altars of all religions since recorded time began, necessitating the organization of huge camel trains to transport the hundreds of tons of frankincense required by the theocratic states of the ancient world. Some idea of how much resin was burnt in the temples can be estimated from Herodotus's report that fifty-eight tons of it were consumed at a single feast of Bel in Babylon; indeed, the importance of incense in ritual is seen in the standard portrayal of the old priest-kings depicted holding a censer as they make their obeisance to the god. It is recorded that frankincense from South Arabia was being burnt in the Sumerian temples as early as 3000 BC, and it has been used continuously ever since. In fact, only during the formative years of Christianity was incense denounced as a requirement of divine service, and this was because the original Nazarenes rejected all pagan rituals *in toto*. The African Tertullian admits that he is prepared to cover up bad smells by burning what he calls the Arabian gum, but he scorns to believe that his prayers would ascend to heaven faster on clouds of smoke than they would on his own breath. In fact, the early Fathers insisted that the sweetest odour of all was a pure conscience. Some ecclesiasts, in their hatred of such pagan rituals as the censing of temples, go so far as to claim that smoke produced by burning frankincense was only appreciated by those demons and mischief-makers who needed such fumes in order to breathe at all; whereas others preferred the argument that since God was incorporeal, he was also noseless and was therefore incapable of smell. In short, all the Fathers up to the period of Constantine the Great, when Christianity became the official religion of the Empire, condemn the use of incense and condemn it for a most basic reason: the test by which Christians during the pagan period could clear themselves of the accusation of subversion was to burn a pinch of incense before a statue of the Emperor. Incense, therefore, was symbolic of both apostasy and idolatry.

The interdiction against incense was withdrawn, however, once the Church had triumphed over paganism, and the Fathers were again able to condone the use of perfumes and flowers in the ritual of worship. Holiness now became identified with a sweet odour; the Devil and his demons with a terrible stench. So incense came into its own again, and by the tenth century the Arabian product was being burnt in Christian churches, and the caravans were again moving up the Incense Road.

But it was not frankincense alone that brought prosperity to Arabia. An immense trade in oriental luxuries had become a feature of civilized life under Imperial Rome, and among the more exotic imports which had to be brought up the Road for distribution to the cities of the empire were those spices which are still common to our tables. Pepper, cinnamon, cloves, ginger, nutmeg, and sesame, all from Asiatic plants, were as

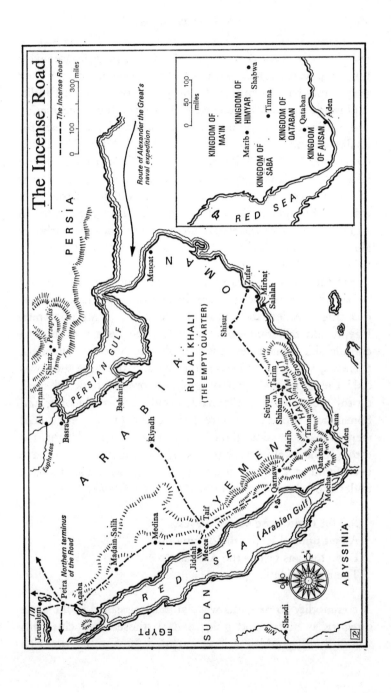

The Incense Road

--- The Incense Road

0   100   300 miles

Route of Alexander the Great's naval expedition

Inset map
KINGDOM OF MA'IN
KINGDOM OF HIMYAR • Shabwa
Marib • Timna • Qataban
KINGDOM OF SABA
KINGDOM OF QATABAN
KINGDOM OF AUSAN • Aden

0   50   100 miles

RED SEA

Main map
PERSIA

Al Qurnah • Shiraz • Persepolis
Basra •
Euphrates
Bahrain •
PERSIAN GULF
Muscat •
Riyadh •
OMAN
Zufar •
Mirbat
Salalah
Shisur •
RUB AL KHALI
(THE EMPTY QUARTER)
A R A B I A
Madain Salih •
Medina •
Taif •
Y E M E N
Seiyun • Tarim
Shibam • HADRAMAUT
Marib • Timna (Incense Groves)
Qarnaw • Qataban Cana
Mocha • Aden
Petra Northern terminus of the Road
Jerusalem •
Aqaba •
Mecca •
Jiddah •
R E D   S E A   (Arabian Gulf)
SUDAN
EGYPT
Nile
Shendi •
ABYSSINIA

familiar to the Roman cook as to twentieth-century housewives; but there were literally scores of other spices whose uses and very names have been forgotten. Aloe-wood from East India, for instance, was once used extensively for perfumes, cosmetics, and medicines; amomum from Malaysia was a spice valued for its flavour and pungency; galanga, native to South China, was considered a cattle medicine as well as a flavour for liqueurs; lakawood, cardamon, cyperus, costum, sweet flag, and dozens of other spices now unobtainable, were available in the street markets throughout the Roman period. All of them came in Arab dhows across the Indian Ocean, were landed at harbours along the South Arabian coast, and loaded on to camels for delivery at Mediterranean ports.

But the main cargoes of the northbound caravans always consisted of frankincense, for in addition to the enormous quantities needed to supply the temples of Mesopotamia, Egypt, and the Mediterranean states, the resin was used in considerable quantities by embalmers, doctors, dentists, chemists, vintners, and cosmeticians; and since the gum was only found in the form of globules on the bark of small thorny trees in the Hadramaut, South Arabia, Socotra, and Somaliland, it became so rare that the tears (as they are called) were even garnered from the beards of goats that had wandered through the frankincense groves. The Elizabethans must have been familiar with the details of the incense trade, to have understood the reference in Shakespeare's *Othello*:

> . . . Of one whose subdu'd eyes,
> Albeit unused to the melting mood,
> Drop tears as fast as the Arabian trees
> Their med'cinable gum . . .

A commodity so precious was naturally classified in the same category as myrrh and gold; and all those tribal chieftains whose South Arabian valleys nurtured the shrub, grew rich and powerful enough to establish their own dynasties. Yet only the names and a jumble of ruins survive to testify to the wealth and importance of such South Arabian kingdoms as Ma'in, Saba, Qataban, Ausan, and Himyar, while today frankincense, the source of their wealth and power, evokes no memories of such petty empires, but rather of the village called Bethlehem to which the three magi brought the royal gifts of gold, frankincense, and myrrh. There is an allusion here, of course, to the ancient trade with the Orient, as in other Biblical references. In fact, the earliest evidence of the existence of the Road is found in the Old Testament account of the Queen of Sheba's mission to King Solomon of Israel around 950 BC. The Queen's caravan, for instance, must have consisted of several hundred camels, 200 being needed to carry the gold alone. Other camels, we are told, were loaded with cargoes of spices and precious stones. Until the French explorer Louis Arnaud reached Marib, the capital of Sheba (Saba), in 1843, the fanciful tale of an immensely rich queen travelling over 1,500 miles in order to compliment Solomon on his wisdom seemed to belong more to the realm of legend than of historical fact. Now we know that a kingdom called Saba not only existed, but that many of its monuments survive and belong with the wonders of the ancient world. The Queen of Sheba, in short, was visiting Jerusalem on a trade and diplomatic mission, and the significance of her journey was not the asking of riddles to test the sagacity of Solomon, but the desire of the Sabaeans to have a strong ally at the northern end of the Incense Road.

The classical Greek geographers tell us that the southern terminal of the Road was a South Arabian seaport called Zufar (perhaps the Zefar of the Bible). Modern historians have been arguing about the location of this place for 200 years or more, as well they might, since the coast along the Gulf of Aden was unexplored and unmapped until well into this century. Explorers had been trying to penetrate Arabia as far back as 1762, when a Danish expedition led by Carsten Niebuhr hoped to

solve the mysteries of the *terra incognita* known to the Romans
as Arabia Felix. Of the six savants who set out, only Niebuhr
returned, and he had never reached the land of frankincense.
Almost 200 years elapsed before any European did, when an
English naval lieutenant, James Wellsted, while surveying the
interior of Oman, brought back a report of a fortified pre-
Islamic town identified by an inscription as Himyarite. The
historians now felt that they were getting nearer to solving the
problem of the legendary kingdoms which had given the
region the name of Arabia the Fortunate; but in the meantime
Oman and the frankincense country in particular had become
more and more isolated and hostile, so that explorers could
not, without great danger and difficulty, bring back any precise
information about the lost cities.

The mystery of what exactly lay behind the mountain ranges
that loom over the Gulf of Aden and the Red Sea had always
puzzled the ancient geographers, and none of them in consequence was able to give a precise account of the interior of
the Arabian peninsula, despite Pliny's list of tribes and the
names of a few towns and villages. True, the Greek merchants
based in Alexandria, Egypt, knew, by the first century AD at
least, the sea route to India via the Red Sea and the Arabian
Sea. They did not know the overland route from the port of
Zufar up to Petra for the very simple reason that the rulers of
the kingdoms along the Incense Road allowed only their own
nationals to control the passage of the caravans. Yet the
hazards of transport via the Red Sea were such that the land
route was preferred for the huge quantities of imported oriental
goods destined for the Western capitals. Significantly, a first
century Greek pilot who described the navigational features
of the Red Sea states that the greater part of the west coast of
Arabia was occupied by 'an evil race of men, so that if a vessel
is driven from her course upon this shore, she is plundered,
and if wrecked, the crew on escaping to land, are reduced to
slavery . . . Moreover, the navigation of this part of the

Local caravans still travel part of the ancient Silk Road across Afghanistan. *Below*: Genghis Khan and Tamerlane fought beneath the walls of Herat, founded by Alexander the Great 2,000 years before the British occupied it and left behind their cannon in the nineteenth century

The Great Wall of China was part of a chain of fortifications built by the emperors to protect their trade routes

An abandoned caravanserai on the Imperial Highway which linked China with the West

Arabian coast is very dangerous; for apart from the barbarity of its people, it has neither harbours nor good roadsteads, and it is foul with breakers and girdled with rocks which render it inaccessible.'[1] The twentieth-century Royal Navy hydrographer who charted this coast nearly 2,000 years later, agrees with his predecessor: the entire Arabian coast, he says, is distinguished by its coral reefs, half-submerged rocks, and banks which sometimes extend as much as fifty miles offshore.

The Incense Road itself was almost as dangerous as the sea route on account of its mountain ranges, tracts of desert, and absence of wells, as the Roman general Aelius Gallus, prefect of Egypt, was to discover when Augustus Caesar ordered him to invade Arabia in 25 BC. Gallus did so with an army of 10,000 legionnaires, 1,000 Nabataean mercenaries from Petra, 500 Jews, 80 warships, 130 transports, and several thousand camels. This formidable expeditionary force crossed the Red Sea, landed on the Arabian coast, and marched southwards. Gallus soon ran into trouble, as any Bedouin could have predicted he would. You cannot move 11,500 soldiers with all their animals across a thousand miles of desert country without courting disaster, especially if you do not know the road and the whereabouts of the wells. The Roman, tricked by his Nabataean guides, floundered about helplessly for months and never did reach the land of frankincense. In fact, he lost almost his entire army with most of his ships; and Arabia Felix remained the exclusive province of the Bedouin, as it has remained to this day.

The task of tracing this first and greatest of the ancient international highways, therefore, has always been immensely difficult for Western travellers, and almost all we know about the Incense Road today is based on the wanderings of individual explorers during the nineteenth and early twentieth centuries—of Arabian travellers like Burckhardt, the discoverer

---

[1] *The Periplus of the Erythraean Sea*, translated by J. W. McCrindle. Calcutta: Thacker, Spink & Co, 1879, p 87.

of Petra, Burton of Mecca, and Doughty of Madain Salih. But
it fell to a modest English couple, Theodore and Mabel Bent,
to explore the frontiers of Arabia Felix and to penetrate inland
from the Oman coast as far as the mountain valleys where the
frankincense groves still flourished.

> It was a most interesting ride along this coast: flat and for
> the most part barren, broken here and there by lagoons of
> brackish and evil-smelling water and mangrove swamps. On
> the way we saw antelopes and foxes with white bushy tails.
> One night we encamped by one of these river beds on
> slightly rising ground, and were devoured by mosquitoes;
> and so pestilent are these insects here that they not only
> attacked us, but tormented our camels to such a degree that
> they were constantly jumping up in the night and making
> such hideous demonstrations of their discomfort, that our
> rest was considerably interfered with.[1]

Theodore and Mabel felt, however, that their trials and tribulations were richly rewarded by their discovery of Lake Khor
Ruri, a tidal lagoon whose exit to the sea had become silted up.

> When we reached the other side of this promontory [Ras
> Risout], to our amazement we saw before us a long sheet
> of water, stretching nearly two miles inland, broken by
> many little creeks, and in some parts fully half a mile wide . . .
> Surely there can be no doubt that this is the harbour which
> was anciently used by the merchants who came to this coast
> for frankincense. It would be absolutely secure at all seasons
> of the year, and it is just twenty parasangs [65 miles] from
> the ruins of the ancient capital—exactly where it ought to be
> in fact.[2]

[1] Theodore Bent and Mrs Theodore Bent, *Southern Arabia*. London: Smith
Elder & Co, 1908, p 269.
[2] *Op cit*, p 271.

Here, the Bents were sure, was the lost city of Zufar, the famous anchorage of the classical period, the port into which came the Arab, Indian, and perhaps even Chinese ships laden with the spices, woods, and precious stones of the East. Here, too, the frankincense was still being brought down from the mountains, to be exported to India in the dhows which had arrived with the winter and would depart with the summer monsoons at the beginning of May—exactly as they had done for 2,000 years, when the pattern of the trade winds in the Indian Ocean had first been mastered. The Bents' theory that Lake Khor Ruri was the harbour called Zufar by the unknown author of *The Red Sea Pilot* (*The Periplus of the Erythraean Sea*), and Abyssapolis by the geographer Ptolemy was to be confirmed seventy years later by an American archaeological team excavating a nearby temple dedicated to one Ilazz, referred to in the ancient histories as King of the Incense Country.

So at least we know where the Road began, as we know where it ended, namely at Petra, the capital city of the Nabataeans, the principal marketers of frankincense and spice. We know, too, that the wealth of Arabia Felix was based entirely on this incalculably rich commerce, to the extent that almost every inhabitant of that country was involved in the rearing and feeding of camels and the organization of the caravans. It was certainly so up to the time of Mohammed and long after—in fact, up to the discovery of oil in this century. Tens of thousands of camels were required to carry an immense tonnage along the tracks which went north from the Hadramaut, the land of the frankincense tree.

Nowadays an enthusiast who had the time, money, and fortitude to follow the Incense Road from its southern end near Mirbat on the coast of Oman to its northern terminal at Petra in Jordan would have to start from Aden in the west or Muscat in the east, for the frankincense country lies roughly midway between these two ports. In the days when South Arabia was partially under the control of a British protectorate at Aden, and partially under that of Turkish governors (though in actual fact it was a strictly tribal territory with the tribes continually feuding among themselves), the only means of reaching Oman was by coastal steamer. These antiquated vessels did not run according to any time-table, nor, for that matter, did they put in at any port along the Dhufar coast, for the simple reason that there were no serviceable ports or deepwater harbours. Those nineteenth-century explorers, like the Bents, who did reach the frankincense country were dependent upon the Arab dhows which still sailed across the Arabian Sea to India, as they had done in the time of Alexander the Great. The Bents were put ashore on the Oman coast in the winter of 1894, to find themselves stranded at the village of Mirbat under the blazing afternoon sun as the Turkish steamer that had brought them disappeared into the distance. Moreover, the villagers were hostile, despite the fact that the English couple had come armed with a letter from Wali Suleiman, the local governor. Nobody seemed very impressed by the use of Wali Suleiman's name and title, and in any case nobody could read the letter. The Bents could only infer that the tribesmen suspected them of having come to interfere with, or spy on, their frankincense monopoly.

However, the travellers were eventually accommodated in the local fort, which they shared with twelve prisoners who wandered about the courtyard as far as the logs of wood or iron bars attached to their legs would permit them. But after the usual delays and confusion, this enterprising pair did set off with a caravan for the Qara mountains and so became the first Europeans to explore the country where the frankincense tree grows. Of course, by the 1890s when the Bents reached the groves, the enormous exports of resin had declined to a point where the trade was no longer of any great commercial value, with only a few hundred tons being collected for shipment to India and hardly any at all going by the old Road up through Arabia to the Mediterranean ports. It was difficult to see why the ancients had called this country Arabia Felix. The Bents found the descendants of the kingdoms of Saba, Qataban, Ma'in, and Hadramaut half-naked cave-dwellers who resembled the 'evil race of men' the old Greek pilot had complained of. Their guides, for example, would not take the travellers where they wanted to go, would march only as long as they saw fit, were unpleasantly familiar, and when asked not to disturb the couple at night deliberately made as much noise as they could.

The character of the Oman and Yemeni tribesmen has not changed all that much to this day, which explains why no Westerner has ever surveyed the full length of the original Incense Road, though an English traveller, Barbara Toy, made a gallant and almost successful attempt to do so in 1967, and this in the middle of the tribal war in Yemen.[1] The difficulties of using the Road because of hostility, suspicion, or religious fanaticism have always meant that a visit to the capitals of the ancient kingdoms—Timna of Qataban, Marib of Saba, Qarnaw of Ma'in—is almost out of the question for the ordinary tourist, though all these cities reveal from their ruined monuments why this country was called Arabia the Fortunate. Small wonder that this fascinating region which produced civilizations as advanced as those of Asia Minor, which built cities of marble and stone when Rome was a village of thatched huts, remains a closed book to all but a few qualified students of ancient Semitic history.

In point of fact, exploration of South Arabia has been so difficult that most of the basic information we do have of these ancient kingdoms has come not from the specialists but from a particular breed of explorer characteristic of the nineteenth century, when Africa and Asia were still almost unknown and unmapped. James Raymond Wellsted (1805–1842) was such a man—not a professional historian at all, but a second lieutenant

[1] Barbara Toy, *The Highway of the Three Kings: Arabia from South to North*. Murray: London, 1968.

aboard the East India Company's survey ship, *Palinurus*, which was engaged in 1834 in charting the South Arabian coast. Wellsted was given permission to wander about between Muscat and Aden, accompanied by his shipmate Lieutenant Whitelock. These two enthusiastic young men travelled with caravans along the fringe of what they called the Great Arabian Desert—that is, the Rub al Khali, or Empty Quarter—but the disturbed state of the country and sickness eventually forced them to work their way back to the coast; and such were the desperate straits that they now found themselves in that Lieutenant Wellsted determined to end his sufferings by discharging both barrels of his shotgun into his mouth. The balls, however, passing upwards, only inflicted two ghastly wounds in his upper jaw. He was finally picked up by an Arab dhow and brought to Bombay, together with his little Arab horse, Sayyid. He survived his Arabian ordeal for only six years, dying in London aged thirty-seven, honoured as a Fellow of the Royal Society for his contributions to the geography and early history of South Arabia.[1]

Lieutenant Wellsted was followed a few years later by another amateur, this time a French pharmacist in the employ of the Imam of Sana. Thomas Arnaud was sponsored by the Société Asiatique on a journey to Marib in order to bring back Himyarite inscriptions from that almost forgotten city. The Frenchman started from the Red Sea port of Jiddah and was not heard of again for a year or more, when the French consular agent at Jiddah received a package containing copies of fifty-six inscriptions and a letter stating that Arnaud had gone blind and was making his way to Aden in the hope of receiving attention from a British physician. He refers to his journey with that modesty displayed time and again by his contemporaries who went alone into dangerous and unknown places:

[1] J. R. Wellsted, FRS, *Travels in Arabia*. London: Murray, 1838.

At Menakhah [he writes] I had to take a guide because the rains were terribly bad and I had lost the sight of my eyes. I have spent six months in a frightful state of blindness, but at the moment, thanks to God, my sight is almost restored.[1]

Arnaud, incidentally, was the first European to reach the Sabaean capital of Marib and to report back on the great dam, now regarded as one of the wonders of the ancient world.

Next to penetrate into the interior was another Frenchman, Joseph Halévy, the Orientalist, who tells us that he completed his explorations 'at the peril of his life', travelling in barbarous regions where no Europeans had ever been—and this as late as 1870, when even the unknown interior of Africa had been to a great extent opened up by European travellers. Halévy had reason to emphasize the hardships he endured and the dangers he overcame, since not only was he, as usual, suspected of some nefarious designs in his search for inscriptions, but he travelled as a Jew among the most fanatical sects of Islam. Eventually, 'a dreadful fever, accompanied by a brain storm, put me within a hand's breath of death,' he writes. 'I had to lie on my bed of pain for a whole month.' No wonder that he employs exclamation marks to express his disgust after he had left his sick bed to visit a large stone near Sana, said to be covered with 'old writings', only to be confronted with an ill-written inscription in Arabic of a couple of verses from the Koran.[2]

Halévy was able to travel from Sana to Marib because, as he says, the caravaners were still using the 3,000-year-old routes. Only now the camels were not carrying spices and frankincense, but the salt mined at Marib. Moreover, the country had lapsed into semi-barbarism so that the Frenchman, as a Jewish merchant, was forced to dismount every time a Moslem

[1] Th. J. Arnaud, *Piéces relatifs aux inscriptions himyarites.* Journal Asiatique, Vol 5, April–May, 1845, p 345. Translation by J. W.

[2] Joseph Halévy, *Rapport sur une mission archeologique dans le Yemen.* Paris: Imprimerie Nationale, 1872, p 48.

passed, meaning that it was simpler for him to walk than to ride. His difficulties were increased by the fear and hatred now felt by true believers towards Israelites, who were regarded as magicians with the power of the evil eye. On one occasion Halévy was refused hospitality in a rest-house on the grounds that the proprietor's cows were in calf and his very presence would cause them to abort. He also gives us a hint as to why the Arabs despised their ancient monuments and hence discouraged all comers from studying them: such monuments, despite—or because of—their obvious superiority to anything that the Bedouin themselves could build, were dismissed as nothing but the manifestations of the pride and rebellion of the *yehoud himyai*, or Himyarite Jews who had, in any case, built them with the aid of demons; and this being so, such monuments were only fit to be destroyed or at best ignored.

But the difficulties and dangers were to some extent alleviated for Halévy (or so he tells us) by the fact that the Arab warriors through whose country he had to pass en route to Marib did not by tradition kill women, unarmed men, or Jews; and so he arrived safely at his destination where he was able to lodge with a Jewish jeweller and to visit the ruins of the famous temples of Saba. Here he secretly copied several hundred inscriptions, taking pains not to let the Arabs see what he was up to, exactly as René Caillié, the first European to reach Timbuctoo and return to tell the tale, had to do in drawing his rough sketches of the fabled African city. Such were the conditions of exploration in the nineteenth century; and one incident that Halévy relates sums up and, indeed, personifies what the traveller had to endure in fanatic Moslem countries.

Having managed after great difficulties to reach Marib, the Orientalist came across a long inscription on a fallen column which he wished to copy. It so happened, however, that the Bedouin women were pounding their washing on this stone, so that when Halévy bent down and began surreptitiously to copy the inscription, bedlam broke loose. He was abused, threatened, and called a sorcerer, at which charge the women howled like furies, the men pointed their rifles at him, and others pummelled him with their fists. The moment had obviously arrived when he was in danger of being murdered; but he stayed calm and turning to the mob, announced that he was a citizen of the holy city of Jerusalem and that his death would inevitably bring misery on his molesters, their children, and their flocks.[1] This threat had an immediate effect. His tormentors left him alone, withdrew outside the door of the temple, and discussed what they should do next. In the meantime, he managed to copy another six lines of the inscription, 'but only in cursive Hebrew characters in order to finish as quickly as possible.' No sooner had the poor man written down his six lines than the Bedouin confiscated his sheet of paper, and so the arguments, yelling, and threats continued until, as suddenly as they had begun, they stopped, and Halévy's principal enemy was inviting him to supper in his tent! Those who have travelled in regions where the old laws and traditions of the desert still obtain will readily understand the happy, if unexpected, ending to this tale.

Joseph Halévy was followed by the Austrian explorer Edward Glaser who made three tremendous journeys into South Arabia between 1882 and 1884, returning eventually to Europe with a collection of 264 Arab manuscripts, 1,032 Himyarite and Sabaean inscriptions (one of which was 130 lines long), and the first accurate map of parts of the Yemen. But after Glaser's visit, the territory of the ancient Arabian kingdoms remained, for all practical purposes, inaccessible to Europeans, with the exception of a handful of Englishmen who identified themselves with the Arab people and their culture. One such was H. St John Philby, friend and adviser to the King of Arabia and a convert to Islam.

It was not until the 1950s that an American expedition

[1] *Op cit*, pp 56 ff.

received permission from the reigning king of Yemen, Imam Ahmed, to dig at ancient Marib; but unfortunately for the archaeologists, the local governor did not recognize the authority of the Imam, but only that of his rival to the throne, Prince Hassan, King Ahmed's brother. The nature and reasons for this tribal feuding were naturally incomprehensible to the American professors, who found themselves continually harassed and spied upon by petty officials, with disastrous results for archaeology. Before long, the six great pillars of the Temple of Bilquis which they had unearthed had toppled like dominoes, some of them being broken in the fall, because the cement required for propping them up had never been delivered. And as a consequence of the collapse, several of the workmen were injured; the expedition photographer was incarcerated in the local jail; the Belgian epigrapher was refused permission to make latex copies of inscriptions; all archaeological finds were confiscated; and soldiers moved into the expedition headquarters. Finally, despite requests to the Imam for an audience, cables to Washington, appeals to the President of the United States, the Secretary General of the United Nations, and the directors of the Foundation for the Study of Man, the expedition leader realized that his position was becoming hopeless, as the hostility of the authorities became more and more ominous. He decided not only to abandon all further digging, but to flee without awaiting permission to stay or to leave, and thus the nineteen members of the expedition managed to escape in their Power Wagons, though only after being chased across the desert by a *goum* of the Yemeni camel corps. The Power Wagons, of course, won the race; the archaeologists lived to tell the tale; and the ruins of Marib were left to sink back into the sand.[1]

The difficulties and, indeed, the dangers of travelling through the kingdoms which flourished along the most

---

[1] The story of this expedition is told in *Qataban and Sheba*, by Wendell Phillips. London: Gollancz, 1955.

ancient of the world's trade routes are probably greater in the 1970s than they were two, or even three, thousand years ago (though this retrogression in the affairs of men is not all that uncommon in the Middle East). There are more frontiers, more barriers, and more obstacles to free travel now than there were in the time of King Solomon. Certainly in Mohammed's day, a learned Jew like Joseph Halévy would not have been harried and despised for his religion, but rather would have been welcomed at every caravanserai for his erudition. It was through the interchange of ideas and the freedom of communication along the Road that desert settlements developed into cities, and primitive peoples became civilized: hence the importance of the Incense Road in the history of mankind. And an interesting aspect of this ebb and flow of cultures is that during the early days of the trade route, civilizing influences moved *up* the Road from South Arabia to the petty principalities of Palestine. Later, the tide of affairs flowed the other way, resulting in the introduction to Arabia of Greek, Roman, Jewish, and eventually Christian ideas. It was this interchange which brought about the most significant and dynamic event in the long history of the Road—the acceptance, first by a small Arabian city, then by almost one third of the world, of the revelations of a caravaner called Mohammed.

Whether Mohammed accompanied *azalai* along the full length of the trade route from Zufar in the south to Petra in the north is not known, but it is unlikely. For whereas a wealthy merchant with an exceptionally valuable cargo might have travelled the entire way to ensure the safety of his goods, in general both camels and cargo went by stages, from one tribe to the next, very much as they do today. Mohammed, who belonged to the Meccan family of Hashim, was a poor orphan without a formal education or business connections and so seemed destined to remain an unknown camel-driver for the rest of his life. But after marrying the wealthy widow Khadiya, whose riches were derived from her husband's caravan interests, he probably became the master of local convoys that plied along the old road between Mecca and Medina.

His companions on his journeys were Greek, Jewish, and Christian travellers, some of whom were scholars, some rabbis, and some priests whose erudition and ideas the illiterate young Arab greatly admired. It was from pondering the long history of religion, from paganism through Judaism to Christianity, that Mohammed created the concept of Islam, or submission to Allah, and was able to formulate a new religion and social creed. He certainly knew the story of the Jews from Abraham to Jesus, though he could not himself read that story in the Bible. Yet the Koran shows a familiarity with both the Old and New Testaments, which he must have acquired from listening to Jews and Christians discussing their beliefs and each trying to prove that their faith offered the best chance of salvation. In this both parties almost succeeded, for Mohammed was prepared to accept both the God of Isaac and of Jesus, and might under the circumstances have been converted to either Judaism or Christianity. As it transpired, he made a kind of synthesis of both religions, superbly adapted to the only world that he knew—the world of the desert and of desert people. He could only have formulated his system at a station on the Incense Road like Mecca, the international meeting-place of Arab, Jewish, Syrian, Greek, and Christian merchants, scholars, and missionaries.

To the majority of caravaners, of course, old and new religions were secondary to the problems of trade. These hard-headed businessmen were not interested in the interchange of cultures. But they made the Road a highway for those who were selling ideas rather than goods, which explains why Christianity reached India before it reached Britain. It explains, too, the eventual collapse of the Road as the foremost trade route of the classical world, since the three rival religions which destroyed paganism—Judaism, Christianity, and Islam—contributed, each in its own way, to the destruction of international trade and the freedom of communication. And by the eleventh century, when Christendom launched the First Crusade, the war of ideas had become a war of men and arms. The conflict has been continued in one form or another up to the present, so that the Middle East in general and Arabia in particular are no longer easily accessible to travellers, and the Incense Road, the first and once the greatest of international highways, has ceased to exist.

5

The Silk Road

An explorer today who wished to survey the whole length of the old Chinese Imperial Highway, popularly known as the Silk Road, would not be permitted to travel east of Balkh in Afghanistan, for the days when men were free to wander about Central Asia, Russian Turkestan, and Western China are over. A journey along the Silk Road, from the 'Jade Gate' at Anhsi on the Chinese frontier to Antioch in Turkey belongs to history, together with the silk caravans of the Han dynasty. This greatest of international highways which once linked the Orient with the West was virtually abandoned soon after Marco Polo passed along it about AD 1251; and the state of international politics being what it is, there is little prospect of it being reopened in this century.

However, for those who see in old roads a kind of microfilm, as it were, of human history, there are vestiges of the Silk Road still visible in friendly countries like Iran and Afghanistan. One of the main arteries of the Road ran across northern Afghanistan and traversed Persia from east to west, and the would-be explorer, provided he can reach the town of Balkh in Afghanistan, will be standing at almost the halfway point along the Road at the junction of the Chinese, Indian, South Russian, and Persian caravans. It was Balkh that Marco Polo described as a 'great and noble city', though the visitor today will be hard put to it to see why. What, indeed, is there to remind him of the ancient prosperity in this strange, deserted place? Certainly nothing survives of the settlement where Zoroaster preached, or of the city where Alexander the

Great married the Persian princess Roxana, for the massive ramparts which still enclose the 'mother of cities' (as the Arabs used to call Balkh) belong to a later period and had probably only been erected shortly before Marco Polo arrived there. And you will find no Greek-speaking people within the walls today, but only a few thousand Afghan herdsmen and traders who occupy a jumble of huts in the midst of acres of ruins. Alexander's city, however, still lives on in the coins which small boys produce from their rags as one wanders along the ramparts, coins minted between 255 BC and 100 BC, when Greek was the official language of Bactria and Greek art and culture penetrated to India and China along the Silk Road. Again, shards of Chinese pottery found lying on the ground under the city walls remind us of those caravans which brought travellers like Hsüan Tsang to Balkh in the seventh century AD, when the city was an international shrine of Buddhism.

Greeks, Kushans, Indians, Persians, and Mongols all captured, destroyed, rebuilt, and occupied Balkh for as long as the silk caravans left China for Europe. Once that lucrative trade ceased, all the cities along the route—Lou-lan, Khotan, Yarkand, Kashgar, Samarkand, Merv, Balkh, Hecatompylos, Palmyra, Antioch—fell into decay and in some cases almost disappeared from the map. Balkh, the 'mother of cities', survived, not as a renowned commercial and religious centre, but as a waste of ruins of interest only to the passing historian.

The Silk Road which brought Balkh its wealth and fame ran almost 5,000 miles from China to the eastern shores of the Mediterranean, the longest international highway in history. Starting in the plains of a country the classical geographers knew only as the 'Land of the Seres', it led across the central Asian deserts, over the Hindu Kush mountain range, and so westward through Asia Minor until it reached the principal ports of the old Phoenician coast. On this enormous journey, the precious bales of silk were transported on the backs of horses, mules, yaks, donkeys, camels, and men by Chinese,

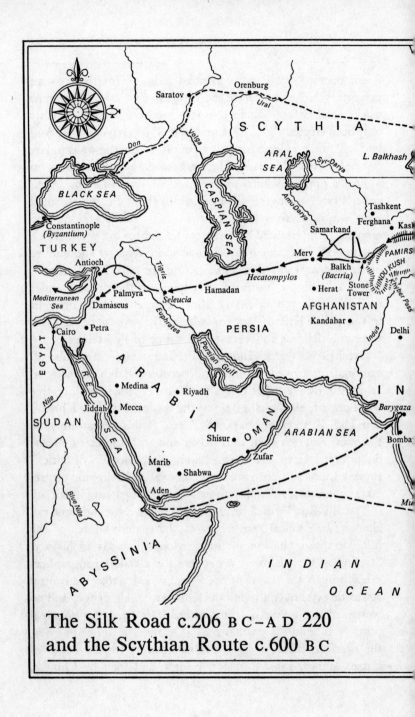

The Silk Road c.206 BC–AD 220
and the Scythian Route c.600 BC

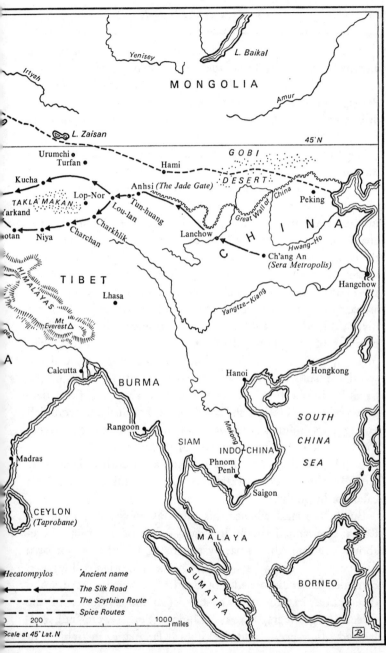

Yenisey

L. Baikal

M O N G O L I A

Irtysh

Amur

L. Zaisan

45°N

Urumchi ●

Turfan ●

Hami

G O B I

D E S E R T

Kucha

Anhsi *(The Jade Gate)*

Peking

TAKLA MAKAN

Lop-Nor

Great Wall of China

arkand

Lou-lan

Tun-huang

C H I N A

otan

Niya

Charchan

Charkhlik

Lanchow

Hwang-Ho

Ch'ang An
(Sera Metropolis)

T I B E T

Hangchow

Lhasa

Yangtze-Kiang

HIMALAYAS

Mt
Everest △

A

Calcutta ●

B U R M A

Hanoi

Hongkong

Rangoon

S I A M

INDO-CHINA

Mekong

S O U T H

C H I N A

S E A

Madras ●

Phnom
Penh

Saigon ●

CEYLON
(Taprobane)

M A L A Y A

B O R N E O

Hecatompylos   *Ancient name*

──◄───   *The Silk Road*

─ ─ ─ ─   *The Scythian Route*

─ ─ ──   *Spice Routes*

200   1000
                                         miles

Scale at 45° Lat. N

Kuchans, Persians, Greeks, Syrians, Jews, and Romans. The merchandise involved was the most valuable and mysterious product of the ancient world: the *serica* of the ancient historians. Perhaps no other commodity, not excluding gold, would have driven men to undertake a journey of such appalling dangers and difficulties.

We do not know, of course, when the first caravans traversed the Silk Road, for the references to 'silk', the country of its origin, and the route by which it reached Rome are few and obscure, whereas in the case of the Incense Road, statements in the cuneiform records as well as in the Old Testament enable us to arrive at specific dates. Further, the Incense Road, the countries it passed through, and the people who controlled it were reasonably well known to the classical geographers, who considered Arabia Felix, and to some extent even India, as part of their own world. China, on the other hand, was a mythical land even to the geographers, since it lay beyond the confines of conquest and exploration. True, the Greeks had given it the name of Seres, from the contemporary Chinese word for silk, and later every Roman matron knew of the Seres by implication whenever she went shopping for a new gown of *sericum*. (What she would get if her husband were rich enough, was a linen garment into which silk had been woven, for not even the wealthiest could afford pure Chinese silk, said to be worth its weight in gold and apparently only actually worn by the emperor Elagabalus when assuming his role of a catamite in public.)

But of the land whence this precious commodity came the Romans remained totally ignorant—even of its exact whereabouts—though this is hardly surprising in view of our own ignorance of that vast country. The historian Pliny who compiled an encyclopaedia of Roman knowledge as it stood during the first century AD stated (on the authority of the Greek geographers) that the Chinese (Seres) were 'tall, red-headed, blue-eyed, and lacking a language in which to communicate their thoughts,' a typical example of pedantic nonsense. He said they harvested the silk for which they were famous from trees, much as cotton is harvested from shrubs. In short, Pliny had no idea whatever of how silk was actually produced, and it can be claimed with some certainty that very few people today are much better informed than the old Roman; or, for that matter, the Greek traveller Plausanias who described the silkworm as an animal about twice the size of a dung-beetle, but more like a spider in appearance on account of its eight legs. This curious creature (he says) was caught by the Seres, kept in a special little house, fed for four years on millet, and finally in its fifth year stuffed with a sort of lettuce, at which stage in its life-cycle it conveniently exploded, allowing the silk thread to be removed from its corpse.

Nobody can say with certainty how or when silk production originated. Legend has it that Lei-tsu, a concubine of the emperor Huang-ti (*circa* 2600 BC), conceived of the possibility of manufacturing silk after studying a silkworm on the mulberry tree making its cocoon. In other words, this observant lady concluded that if a person could reverse the process of spinning as performed by the industrious worm, he (or more likely she) would be able to unravel a thread which, despite its gossamer quality, was strong enough to be woven into yarn for use as a fabric. Lei-tsu and her associates soon discovered, however, that there were two problems which had to be solved before the manufacture of silk was practicable; and it was the solution of these two problems, no doubt as a result of years, perhaps centuries, of experiment, which constituted the secret of sericulture and gave the Chinese a monopoly of silk manufacture for some 2,500 years.

The first problem was how to avoid breaking the thread which enshrouds the caterpillar in its pupal state, for in order to unravel a continuous thread the cocoon must not be pierced or damaged in any way. The second problem was how to 'domesticate' the silkworm, since the care and cultivation of this animal from the egg stage to the completion of the cocoon could not be left entirely to nature if silk was to be produced in quantity as well as quality.

The Chinese solved the second problem by treating the silk-worm with the care usually given in the West only to pedigree animals. It was raised from the egg in a fixed temperature, free from the heat of the midday sun and the cold of the night; it was fed on finely chopped white mulberry leaves gathered every half-hour; it was protected from draughts, loud noises, unpleasant smells, and unwashed attendants. And when the caterpillar, gorged to satiety and its weight increased five thousand-fold, decided to get to work, it was placed in a clean litter of rice straw and stimulated to spin by gently raising the temperature. The result was a cocoon containing an average of 1,000 yards of thread.

The problem of how to unwind this thread was now solved by plunging the cocoon into boiling water in order to kill the pupa without damage and to dissolve at the same time the sericin, or gum, which cements the silk filaments together. The next step in this long and careful process was to stir the boiling water with twigs, in which the cocoons were caught, to be placed in a tray ready for unravelling. Finally, great skill was needed to unwind the thread, and girls with the most delicate touch were employed for this purpose. The usual practice was to join and twist together the threads of several cocoons; and once this was accomplished, the strands could be united to produced yarns of various weights, transparency, and strength. Thus, some 3,000 years ago, when most Europeans were still devoid of almost all sophisticated skills, the Chinese had discovered how silkworms could be domesticated, how to select and sort the emerging cocoons for colour and quality, and how to join as many as twenty filaments to make a single strand, from which the silk brocades and gauzes were produced on looms.

It follows that such an extraordinarily beautiful fabric was of immense value, and even in China, where sericulture had become a thriving industry by the time of the Han dynasty (206 BC–AD 220), silk was the exclusive cloth of the Imperial families. At the same time the inventive and resourceful Chinese discovered that silk had a hundred uses other than as a luxury fabric—as a string for musical instruments or weapons like the bow, a line for fishing rods, an ingredient of fine paper, a container for packaged goods, even a substitute for china-ware (for example, they made cups of lacquered silk). So gradually the production of silk was stepped up until supply actually exceeded demand inside China, and the surplus silk began to find its way, though quasi-illegally, across the frontiers to the outside world. And when the Chinese merchants and all those engaged in the caravan trade dis-covered that this silk was worth far more than its weight in gold, the Silk Road became one of the busiest highways of the classical world.

Actually the Silk Road was not established for trading pur-poses only, nor were the Chinese emperors themselves involved in selling their silk or anything else to the West. To them the Road was essentially a military highway, comparable with the great Roman roads which connected the legion outposts with the capital. The origin and maintenance of this long line of communication were due to the Chinese need for *horses*, not the West's need for silk. The horses in question were described by the general Chang Ch'ien in 140 BC as 'superb horses which sweat blood when they perspire'.[1]

Why did they need horses and why did they set so much store by the Iranian breed which Chang had seen in and around Ferghana in eastern Turkestan? The answer is that Imperial China from the time of unification under the Ch'in dynasty (221–206 BC) was always in danger from the Huns

---

[1] This 'blood-sweating' is not, of course, a reference to 'blood' horses like the Barbs and Arabians, but is a literal description of bleeding caused by a parasite burrowing under the shoulder and causing blisters which burst and oozed blood.

who, as barbarians and nomads, lived by raiding and looting. To fight and contain these fast-moving barbarians, the Chinese needed a new breed of war-horse. And so the emperor Han Wu-ti sent General Chang to the West across territory which had never been visited by any official of the Chinese government before expressly to barter for the so-called 'celestial horses' which were able to carry heavily-armoured men for long distances across rough country.

Chang Chi'en arrived back in China thirteen years after he had set out, and was loaded with honours, even though he had been unable to bring back any blood-sweating horses. But he had pioneered a road to the West and seen for himself that trade was possible with kingdoms thousands of miles beyond the Great Wall. Not that the emperors were interested in enriching themselves by trade; they were able to do that much more simply by exacting tribute from their provinces. But Chinese officials, merchants, bankers, tradesmen, porters, and all those who lived by commerce of one sort and another were quick to take advantage of the opening of the West, now that diplomatic relations had been established with the Hellenized countries of Western Asia and, through them, with the Mediterranean world. In short, it was the Chinese who joined Europe to the Orient and who pioneered the Silk Road which linked the Pacific with the Atlantic Ocean.

As the silk caravans began to arrive at the great depots of Antioch, Damascus, Palmyra, and Petra, the Romans grew more curious about the country whence this most precious of products originated. But this curiosity was limited to a small group of Greco-Roman intellectuals specializing in geography and cartography: the ordinary citizens seem to have had no interest in the peoples or countries beyond the confines of their own towns. Roman officials in particular were surprisingly parochial in this respect and seem to have regarded the world beyond the Mediterranean as a wilderness inhabited by monsters. They relied on military reconnaissance only for an assessment of new territories and left the gathering of any other geographical information to merchants, caravan guides, sea-captains, and occasional travellers. Consequently geographers like Strabo, Pomonius Mela, Pliny, Dionysius Periegetes, Marinus Tyrius, and Ptolemy, all of whom were intensely curious about the whereabouts of the Land of Silk, had very few hard facts indeed to go on and actually all copy from one original source, repeating the same or similar errors, so that even by the end of the second century AD, at least 400 years after silk had become a fairly common luxury article throughout Roman Europe, the silkworm was thought to be that spider-like creature which blew itself up by over-eating.

As for the route by which the silk arrived from the East, the only factual information available to the geographers, and hence to the public, was first published in a treatise by Marinus of Tyre about AD 100. Marinus was a Greek intellectual living in the thriving commercial port of Tyre where he had the opportunity of talking to the caravan masters and ship-captains and of studying the itineraries of travellers. One of his most valuable sources of geographical information was the log-book of one Maes Titianus, a Macedonian merchant banker who appears to have financed and organized a sort of private East India Company, an import-export enterprise dealing in oriental goods. Maes was particularly interested in getting a monopoly of the trade if he could, for already in the reign of Augustus silk garments were being sold in fashionable shops in Rome and the principal Italian cities; and so fashionable did it become that the contemporary moralists were soon inveighing against it because it 'revealed more of a woman's naked charms than it concealed'. Presumably they had the same objection to the wearing of silk by men, since this practice had to be prohibited by law in AD 30—a law which did not really affect the silk trade.

At all events, Maes Titianus sent out commercial travellers to make a survey of the route with particular attention to the

main caravanserais where it would have been profitable for his
company to set up an agency. From the reports brought back
by his travellers, classical geographers were able to draw their
tentative maps of the world beyond the Khyber Pass. It is also
Maes's *itinerarium* which enables us to chart the Silk Road
roughly from its western terminus in Antioch to its Chinese
base in Ch'ang An. It runs from Antioch to Palmyra, down the
Euphrates to Seleucia (twenty miles south-east of Baghdad),
across Persia to Antiochia Margiana (Merv, or Mary, in Soviet
Central Asia, believed in Hindu, Parsi, and Arab tradition to
be the ancient Paradise), thence to Bactria (now Balkh in
northern Afghanistan) until it reached a mysterious Stone
Tower, identified by many historians with Tash Kurgan,
located near the Chinese–Russian border on the eastern side
of the Pamirs. The Stone Tower seems to have been regarded
as the boundary between Europe, Euroasia, and the true Orient,
for evidently the agents of Maes Titianus did not proceed beyond this point. We know where the road went after the Stone
Tower, however, from Chinese sources, clarified by the surveys
of explorers like Sir Aurel Stein, Sir Erich Teichman, Sven
Hedin, and Peter Fleming. From the Tower it ran to Kashgar,
an oasis on the western edge of Takla Makan, the desert used
by the Chinese for their atomic explosions. From Kashgar one
route went north around the desert, another to the south of it,
the two roads linking up at Anhsi in Western China, and so
eastward via Lanchow to Ch'ang An in the Shensi province.
Ch'ang An is thought to be the Sera Metropolis of the Greek
geographers.

The principal obstacles to travel along the Silk Road have
always been as much political as physical, whether in the
second century BC or the twentieth century AD, though the
problems of journeying in Central Asia are too ephemeral to
discuss here. Who now, for instance, is interested in the
struggle for power between local tribes like the Turkis,
Kirghiz, Tungans, Kazaks, Tajiks and so forth; or in the

Women selecting silkworms which are ready to spin. One of a series of drawings of Chinese silk culture and manufacture, dated the 35th year of Emperor K'ang H'si

careers of the *Wang* (or Prince) of Hami, Governor Yang Tseng-hsin, General Ma Chung-ying and the rest?[1] The equivalent of these tribes and these warlords existed during the great days of the Road, and the wars in which they were involved were much the same. But despite all the problems, political and geographical, despite wars, revolutions, and

[1] For the local disturbances with which explorers had to contend, see the books by Sir Aurel Stein, Sir Eric Teichman, Owen Lattimore, Peter Fleming, Sven Hedin, and other travellers who followed the Silk Road in parts before 1940.

natural calamities, the bales of silk got through and continued to do so for centuries. The reason was that a tacit understanding obtained all along the trail that the caravans should be allowed to pass—provided, of course, the usual dues and bribes were paid, such dues and bribes being systematized today in our Customs and Excise. The Road, although always extremely hazardous, not least on account of the terrain itself (deserts, swamps, high mountains) but also because of bandits and highwaymen, was never closed during the continual Middle Eastern wars of the Roman period; and the vague agreement between the monarchs and tribes through whose territory the trade passed somehow survived the perpetual chaos characteristic of barbarians. The road was not only kept open, but it was protected and served by military outposts, caravanserais, wells, and watch-towers, some of which survive today in the remotest places. Indeed, the Chinese achievement in the field of communications equals that of the Romans, both peoples using almost precisely the same art and science to keep open and secure the trade routes used by the caravans. Their engineers, for instance, constructed paved roads, stone bridges, and post stations across thousands of miles of wild and dangerous country; and just as it became possible for a British citizen of the third century AD to travel from York to Rome in comparative comfort and safety, so the Chinese merchant of the Han period (206 BC–AD 220) could transport his cargo of silk from the 'Jade Gate' on the western frontier of the Chinese empire to the eastern border of Imperial Rome. And the Chinese sections of this caravan route were in no wise inferior to the Roman, though the terrain the oriental convoys had to cross was much more formidable than anything the Romans met with in Europe. But with the collapse of a strong central Chinese government, whole stretches of the Silk Road had to be abandoned as the garrisons were overrun, the road stations destroyed, caravanserais looted, and cultivation of the oases brought to a standstill. All that remains today of the Road that begins at the 'Jade Gate' are the ruins of Chinese watch-towers that run for miles across deserts and salt-marshes and, in places, the vestiges of the extension to the Great Wall itself. Sir Marc Aurel Stein, who was to discover the Chinese terminus of the Road, describes the scene in these words:

> Never did I feel more the strange fascination of this desolate border than while I thus traced the remains of wall and watch-stations over miles and miles of bare desert and past the salt-marshes . . . As I sat amidst the debris of the small watch-room usually provided to shelter the men on guard and let my eyes wander over this great expanse of equally desolate marsh and gravel, it was easy to recall the dreary lives once passed here . . . Struck by the rays of the setting sun, tower after tower, up to ten miles distant or more, could be seen glittering as if the plaster coating which their walls had once carried were still intact. How easy it was then to imagine that towers and walls were still guarded.[1]

The British explorer was some 5,000 miles from Northumber-land when he wrote these words, but he could easily have been sitting amidst the debris of a mile castle on Hadrian's Wall, so similar was the military architecture of the Chinese and Roman emperors.

The watch-towers and the walls were not sufficient to keep out China's ancient enemies, the barbarous Huns against whom the Great Wall, which had taken eighteen years (*circa* 240–222 BC) and the labour of 3,000,000 soldiers to build, had been the only barrier; and when successive Chinese dynasties succumbed to their own internal dissensions or to external invaders, the end came in 1213 AD with the invasion and conquest of the Mongols. To Genghis Khan and his sons, China was intended to be nothing more than a pasture for

[1] Sir M. A. Stein, *On Ancient Central-Asian Tracks*. London: Macmillan, 1933, pp 184, 185.

their horses. The once lucrative international trade between China and the West was finished, not only with the collapse of the Road, but because the lifeblood of that trade, the raw silk produced for a thousand years exclusively in Chinese factories, was now being manufactured in Europe. The mysterious fabric, like the mysterious creature that made it, was no longer a secret; by the middle of the sixth century AD, sericulture had been brought to Europe.

As one would half expect, the manner of its coming to Europe was as mysterious as its origin in China. The legend says that it was first brought to the central Asian kingdom of Khotan by a Chinese princess, the bride of the king of that country. The eggs of the silkworm were hidden in her hair. And by the sixth century AD, sericulture was being practised as far west as Syria, though it was not yet known in the Roman territories. According to Procopius, the Byzantine historian, the long-kept secret was revealed to Justinian by two monks who had returned from a country Procopius calls Serinda. The emperor immediately dispatched agents disguised as merchants who eventually managed to bring back both silkworm eggs, and equally important, specialists to start scientific sericulture in the West. From this time onwards, the secret of the silkworm was known throughout the civilized world. The great centres of manufacture were to be in Spain, Sicily, Italy, and France.

It follows that once the Chinese had lost their monopoly in silk, the long and arduous road which was the main artery of trade between East and West lost its importance. The great caravans which had set out from the 'Jade Gate' in the time of Ch'in and Han were reduced now to a few merchants dealing principally in spices and gums, still much prized in the West, as products like ginger are to this day. However, the Road remained the main highway between the continents and was still used by long-distance as well as local caravans and by pilgrims, diplomats, and merchant-adventurers. Among the latter were the Polo brothers who were accompanied by Marco, the son of one and the nephew of the other. These three Venetians set out about 1250 to visit Cathay, as China was now known to Europeans. Their primary mission was to bring Kubilai Khan, grandson of Ghengis Khan, greetings from the Christian Pope, for the Mongol emperor was said to be as interested in all religions as he was in all the sciences and arts. And in order to reach Kubilai, who had established his court at Peking, the Venetians took the old Silk Road via the Pamirs, Kashgar, Yarkand, Khotan, and Lop-Nor, all strategic places familiar to Chinese travellers, but completely unknown to Europeans until Marco Polo passed through them in 1270. One can understand why these towns and regions were *terra incognita* on reading the descriptions by ancient as well as modern travellers of such areas as the Takla Makan desert, which lies between the Pamirs and western China and which the caravans had to by-pass either to the north or south. The Takla Makan, indeed, has the reputation of being the most terrible desert of all, though the traveller who has crossed the Sahara sand seas would not necessarily agree. But Marco's description written seven centuries ago is still evocative:

> The length of this desert is so great that it is said it would take a year and more to ride from one end of it to the other. [It is actually about 600 miles at its greatest length.] It is all composed of hills and valleys of sand, and not a thing to eat is to be found on it.
>
> There is a marvellous thing related of this desert, which is that when travellers are on the move by night, and one of them chances to lag behind or to fall asleep, or the like, when he tries to gain he will hear spirits talking and will suppose them to be his comrades. And in this way many have perished.[1]

[1] *The Book of Ser Marco Polo . . .*, translated and edited by H. Yule. London: Murray, 1871, pp 103, 104.

With the publication of Marco Polo's *Travels* at the beginning of the fourteenth century, the West at last had a glimpse of the mysterious Land of the Seres and of the way thither. At first nobody quite believed the narrator who had earned for himself the soubriquet of *milioni* on account of his frequent use of grand numerical expressions. But there was no denying that he had given a detailed description of his journey along the Silk Road across almost the whole breadth of Asia, with kingdom after kingdom, region after region, tribe after tribe, carefully documented. There had been nothing even faintly resembling his discoveries since the expedition to India of Alexander the Great, for Marco Polo had opened up an entirely new world, not only the world of China, but of the Pacific Ocean. He was, in short, the first European to report the existence of Burma, Laos, Siam, Japan, Java, Sumatra, and the islands of the archipelago, and the first to give any comprehensive account of the mysterious Christian empire of Abyssinia. His fantastic journey was the beginning of a new era.

The first to follow in the Venetian's footsteps were priests and monks sent to China by the Popes, who had taken a keen interest in that country ever since it had been rumoured that the Mongols were interested in becoming Christians. Indeed, Kubilai Khan had requested the Pope (whom he understood to be 500 years old) to send him about a hundred missionaries and a flagon of sacred oil from the Holy Sepulchre. This looked like an auspicious beginning to relationships between the Orient and the West; but the ecclesiasts had scant knowledge of the Mongol mentality, not realizing that Kubilai wanted 'missionaries' to act as advisers and teachers while probably assuming that the holy oil was another remedy for rheumatism. Nonetheless, this amazing man, who ruled from 1259 for thirty-five years over the largest empire mankind has ever known, was genuinely interested in every branch of knowledge, including theology. It appears that he found the disputations between the exponents of Confucianism, Buddhism, and

Islam entertaining, so he was not averse to adding a Christian apologist to his retinue. At the same time, he was shrewd enough to appreciate the technological superiority of the West, and willingly accepted the services of captives and adventurers who had reached China by one route or another. We hear, for instance, of a German armourer who was employed to manufacture a catapult called the mangonel; of a Russian goldsmith who cast the imperial throne; of a Russian linguist who was the official translator; of a French sailor who was the royal tent-maker; of a Greek renegade who was employed as a spy; and of a German girl who was used as a sort of priestess by the diviners. But all these Europeans were prisoners of war and had been taken to China by force, whereas the monks and merchants were guests at Kubilai's court in Peking. As a result, this period, 1259–1294, was the golden age of East-West relations, a period of which it was said that a young girl carrying a golden vessel on her head could walk right across Asia without being molested. That this was not wholly an exaggeration is proved by the reports of the merchants who used the trans-Asian routes, including the old Silk Road. We are told by Francesco Pegolotti, the Florentine commercial agent and author of *Practice of Marketing*, that these routes were 'perfectly safe, whether by day or night.' However, with the death of Kubilai Khan in 1294 and the overthrow of the Mongol dynasty in 1368, the old anarchy prevailed again throughout Central Asia, a state of affairs that has continued up to the present day. The great highway which had linked China with Rome, and hence the Pacific with the Atlantic was, for purposes of international intercourse, closed once and for all; and like the Incense Road across Arabia, it was never to be reopened. It continued, of course, to be used for local trade, and the traveller in northern Iran, Afghanistan, Uzbekistan (USSR), and the western provinces of China[1] will occasionally

[1] It is highly unlikely, however, that a traveller would be allowed to wander about freely in either the Russian or Chinese territories.

see a small caravan moving parallel to the line of the old road, which is now partially paved in the Communist territories. But the silk caravans, of course, have long since ceased, perhaps the last of any size being a caravan of nearly a thousand camels which arrived in Samarkand in 1404.

Alas for the history of mankind, the friendly and mutually beneficial ties which kings like Kubilai Khan and Popes like Gregory X had cemented between East and West, were so strained by wars, local as well as international, that land communications between Europe and China ceased altogether by the end of the fifteenth century, necessitating the discovery of a new route to the Indies. Such a route was, in fact, absolutely essential to the West, which had relied on oriental spices and drugs since Roman times; and if any proof of this fact were needed, we have the evidence of Columbus's daring voyage *westward* in the hope of reaching China and Indonesia. Eventually the circumnavigation of Africa by the Portuguese navigators opened the sea-route to the Far East, after which European trade with the Orient was conducted almost entirely by sea, so that the China of the Silk Road and of Marco Polo and of the Franciscan friars and the Christian communities they established and of the Italian merchants with their warehouses disappeared from the pages of history. Europeans were soon to be almost as ignorant of China as they had been in the reign of Augustus Caesar; and it would have been almost impossible to find anybody in Elizabethan England who would have believed that many Chinese cities were far larger, richer, and more magnificent than London: that Hangchow, the old Sung capital, for instance, had been the largest city in the world for centuries.

With the end of the Mongol and the beginning of the Chinese Ming dynasty in 1368, China turned her back on the despised foreigners, both monks and merchants, and from this time onwards the old Land of Silk became *terra incognita* to Westerners. Apart from the spice trade which was still enormous, Chinese and Europeans had little in common and, for that matter, still do. Historians and geographers were anxious to fill in the enormous gaps in their knowledge of this vast territory with the biggest population of any country on earth, but the difficulty was one of communication, not simply of language either, but of culture. One has only to read the descriptions of China by nineteenth-century travellers to appreciate this difficulty and to understand where the music-hall caricature of the 'Chinaman' with his pigtail and pidgin-English originated. The problems of exploring the Silk Road that were enormous a century ago are almost insuperable today. Fortunately for those fascinated by the story of this fabulous highway, the nineteenth century provided a breed of explorers who were seldom discouraged by physical obstacles and who combined great powers of endurance with remarkable erudition—men and women who travelled their chosen road with the relevant Greek, Latin, Chinese, and Arabic texts in their baggage, together with sextant, transits, and theodolites. From the discoveries of these travellers, we are able to trace the Silk Road across regions which have always been virtually closed to outsiders.

The greatest of these Asian explorers was Sir Marc Aurel Stein, the British archaeologist and geographer who was born in Budapest, Hungary in 1862, died in Kabul, Afghanistan in 1943, and was seldom in Britain at all. In fact, most of his adult life was spent in the deserts and mountains of Central Asia, following the Silk Road in the footsteps of his beloved Hsüan Tsang, the Chinese Buddhist pilgrim who in the seventh century AD travelled from his convent in China, alone and without resources across the Gobi desert to Samarkand. He was not to return to his homeland until fifteen years later, when he dictated to his disciples the narrative of his fabulous travels in a book which accompanied Aurel Stein on all his expeditions. It was along Hsüan Tsang's road, in fact, that Stein discovered the walled-up Temple Library at the Cave of

6

the Thousand Buddhas, perhaps the greatest find ever made by a Westerner in Asia:

> The day was cloudless and hot [he writes], and the 'soldiers' who had followed me about during the morning with my cameras were now taking their siesta in sound sleep soothed by a good smoke of opium.
> The priest had now summoned up courage to open before me the rough door closing the narrow entrance into the rock-carved recess. The sight of the small room disclosed was one to make me open my eyes wide. Heaped up in layers, but without any order, there appeared in the dim light of the priest's little lamp a solid mass of manuscript bundles rising to a height of nearly ten feet and filling, as subsequent measurement showed, close on 500 cubic feet.[1]

Aurel Stein's account of how he tried to obtain this entire collection of ancient Buddhist manuscripts for forty horse-shoes, with which the temple priest would have been able to take off to his native province and live in some luxury 'should things become too hot for him', is the classic story of all explorers in remote and primitive places where beautiful ruins, temples, and monasteries bespeak a splendid past. The fact is that old manuscripts are of no value to peasants, and the rescue of them and of all the artefacts from the golden age of Buddhism by Sir Aurel was wholly justified. After him, very few explorers indeed were able to travel the Silk Road. One of the last of them, the Swede Sven Hedin, personified the end of an era, the era of the caravan, for by the 1920s, Hedin was travelling across the Gobi desert by lorry and motor car. In fact, the Swedish explorer had been commissioned by the Chinese government to 'turn the old Imperial highway or Silk Road into a modern motor road'.[2] This being China of the

---

[1] M. Aurel Stein, *Ruins of Desert Cathay*. Macmillan: London, 1912, Vol 2, p 172.
[2] Sven Hedin, *The Silk Road*. London: Routledge, 1938, p 13.

war-lords, however, nothing of the kind was accomplished; once China was unified under the Communists, modernization, industrialization, and total rejection of the past as the hated age of imperialism, ordained the end of the Silk Road. Sven Hedin wrote its epitaph some fifty years ago when he had finished his survey of this once great highway:

> We saw the Great Wall which, mile after mile and day after day, lay stretched across the desert like an endless yellow snake, having discharged its duty of protecting the Central Empire against the barbarians. And we saw the innumerable watch-towers which rose by the wayside, dumb and yet eloquent witnesses to a vanished time of greatness. . . And we saw the Silk Road at its lowest ebb, with dormant life and dying trade, the connecting towns and villages in ruins and the population languishing in a state of permanent insecurity and miserable poverty. Only in our imagination did we see the brilliant, many-coloured scenes from the past, the unbroken carnival of caravans and travellers.[1]

[1] *Ibid*, p 230.

The African Caravans—Gold

There survives in the Fezzan in Libya a caravan route which we know has been in use since the beginning of recorded history. This road runs along a valley called the Wadi el Ajal, once the heartland of a mysterious North African tribe called the Garamantes. Herodotus has a famous reference to these people as chariot-riders, and they appear from time to time in the Roman histories. But well before the arrival of the Garamantes on the scene, the Wadi el Ajal was being travelled and settled by races who left a record of themselves behind in the form of various monuments and artefacts.

The evidence begins with rock paintings and engravings found on the sides of the sandstone cliffs which enclose the Wadi for miles along its southern flank. The oldest of these pictures goes back to 15,000 BC, when this region of the Sahara was covered in woods and watered by rivers, and animals like the extinct *bubalus antiquus*, or wild buffalo, roamed through the valleys along with antelopes, giraffes, ostriches, monkeys, and aquatic animals seldom found nowadays in Africa north of the Tropic of Cancer. The tribesmen who lived on the sides of the cliffs along the Wadi el Ajal must have observed these animals from their eyries, since they drew them by the thousand on rock faces all over the Sahara. The artist-hunters were succeeded, as the rock paintings show, by herdsmen with domesticated cattle. A regular caravan route connecting the Niger River valley with the Mediterranean ports of the North African littoral had not yet been established, though probably by this time, 500 BC, some form of local trade had begun between those groups who had permanent settlements along the valley. Yet since they had no beasts of burden—neither donkeys, horses, nor camels—we cannot yet speak of organized caravans. But when we find, as we do in the still-unexplored Acacus Mountains of southwest Fezzan, pictures of the Garamantes' horse-drawn carts (the so-called 'flying chariots'), we can at least speculate on the origins of long-distance trade; and once the first crude drawings of camels appear, we can be sure that such a trade was firmly established. These pictures are primary evidence of caravan traffic, for it seems that travellers in the desert have always wanted to commemorate their passing on the rocks beneath which they camped at the end of the day. The thousands of inscriptions in Arabic and Tifinagh on the smooth faces of boulders throughout the Sahara are the memorials of the last thousand years of the desert caravaners.

Despite the certainty that the Carthaginians, and after them the Romans, were trading with central Africa, using the Way of the Garamantes which followed the Wadi el Ajal for that purpose, it is of little use attempting to trace the African trade routes before the arrival of the Arabs in the seventh century AD and the introduction by the Bedouin of the camel. Both events were of supreme importance in history, first because, as a result of the Arab conquests, Islam became the religion of almost the entire upper half of Africa, wiping out almost every trace of Christianity, which, up to that time, had been the official religion; and secondly, because large long-distance caravans were made possible by the camel. From now on the African trade was one of the richest in the world. It was based on the transport of gold, salt, and slaves.

A trickle of gold had been coming out of West Africa since Carthaginian times, though nobody knew the location of the mines, except that they were somewhere south of the Sahara. Even the Arabs, who within a hundred years of their conquest of Roman Africa had crossed the Sahara to trade with the

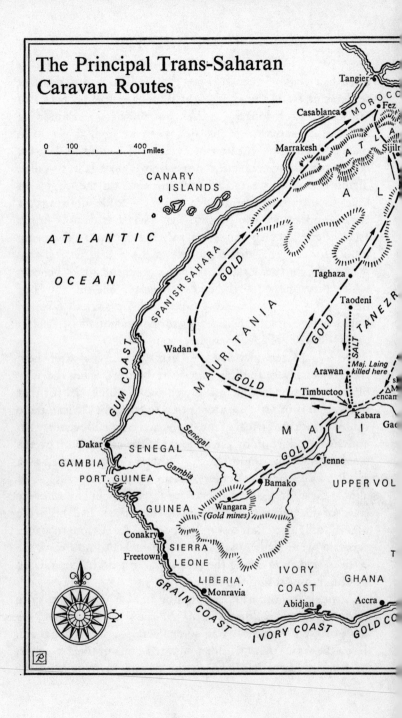

The Principal Trans-Saharan Caravan Routes

0 100 400 miles

CANARY
ISLANDS

ATLANTIC

OCEAN

Tangier

MOROCC

Casablanca

Fez

Marrakesh

Sijilr

ATLA

AL

L

SPANISH SAHARA

GOLD

MAURITANIA

Taghaza

GOLD

Taodeni

SALT TANEZR

Wadan

GOLD

Arawan

Maj. Laing
killed here

GOLD

Timbuctoo

sl
M
encam

Kabara

Gac

GUM COAST

Dakar

SENEGAL

Senegal

MALI

GOLD

Gambia

Jenne

GAMBIA

PORT. GUINEA

Bamako

UPPER VOL

GUINEA

Wangara
(Gold mines)

Conakry

SIERRA

Freetown

LEONE

IVORY

COAST

GHANA

LIBERIA

Monravia

Accra

Abidjan

GRAIN COAST

IVORY COAST

GOLD CO

T

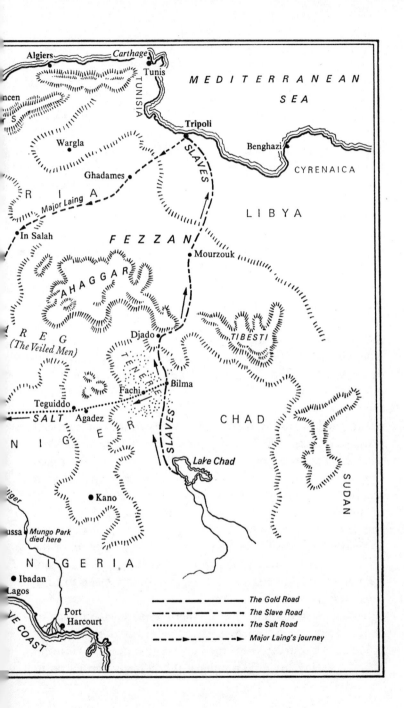

Algiers   Carthage
Tunis

MEDITERRANEAN
SEA

ncen

TUNISIA

Tripoli

Wargla

Benghazi

CYRENAICA

Ghadames

R
I
A

Major Laing

A

LIBYA

In Salah

FEZZAN

Mourzouk

HAGGAR

REG
(The Veiled Men)

Djado

TENERE

TIBESTI

Teguiddo

Fachi

Bilma

SALT

Agadez

G

E

R

CHAD

Lake Chad

N
I

Kano

SUDAN

ussa Mungo Park
died here

NIGERIA

Ibadan

Lagos

Port
Harcourt

VE COAST

——————————	The Gold Road
—·—·—·—·—·—	The Slave Road
··················	The Salt Road
— — —▶— — —▶	Major Laing's journey

Sudan, could never in the beginning discover the exact location of these mines, though eventually travellers were to bring back tales of naked gold-miners who lived in holes in the ground and only emerged to heap little piles of gold at the edge of the shafts where the Arab traders placed their goods for exchange. When both parties were satisfied, the miners withdrew down their shafts and the merchants rode off on their camels.

These reports greatly puzzled Western observers. Where were these mines? And what was all this about troglodytes disappearing down holes in the ground? Every new account seemed more contradictory and confusing. Some said that the gold sprouted in the sand in the form of carrots. Others that it grew like coral . . . It travelled along tunnels underground . . . It was harvested by ants the size of cats. (This last version was the accepted one at the beginning of the fourteenth century, when the monk, Richard of Haldingham, drew his famous Map of the World, still to be seen in Hereford Cathedral, depicting cat-size ants on the western coast of Africa.) In addition to the mystery as to whether the gold grew like a vegetable or proliferated like coral, there were reports of the miners themselves who, according to one account, were said to be maidens who drew up the gold dust from the mud of a lake called Cyraunis with the aid of birds' feathers smeared with pitch; but according to another, were men 'very black in colour . . . [with] the lower lip, more than a span in width, hanging down, huge and red, over the breast, displaying the inner part glistering like blood'—a possible reference to the African custom of the lip disc. In fact, nearly all the stories told about the mines and the miners, however fantastic they may sound, seem to have some basis in fact.

It was not until quite recently that the myths and mysteries of the African gold mines were explained and resolved. In 1960 two English explorers reached a region near the Guinea–Mali frontier where gold-mining was still being carried on in almost exactly the same way as when the first Arabs visited the area some 1,200 years before. They found that the methods used to extract the gold entailed digging holes three to five feet apart to a depth of about forty feet. The miners next lowered themselves to the bottom of these shafts and connected them by means of lateral tunnels. Squatting inside these three-foot-high tunnels up to his waist in water, the miner hacked out lumps of gold-bearing quartzite, which he placed in a large calabash and sent floating along the gallery to the bottom of the shaft, where a worker gave the quartzite the first washing before sending it up to the surface in another calabash (the first having been floated back to the face-worker). Here the ore was heaped into piles to await the coming of the women in the afternoon. It was the women who completed the washing by standing knee-deep in pools of water swirling the calabashes round and round until the dross had been washed away and a few grains of gold dust remained in the receptacle. The whole operation, like similar operations in the open salt mines of Bilma and Teguiddo, is a family business in which each miner of the tribal group has his or her special and traditional function: the skilled men mine in the tunnels; their young sons keep the 'assembly line' of calabashes moving; other relations haul the pay dirt to the surface; wives and daughters do the final wash; the tribal chief directs operations and collects the daily yield; and the men too old to work underground act as salesmen to the itinerant merchants.[1]

One can see from this description of central African gold-mining how the legends about troglodytes inhabiting holes in the ground originated and multiplied. Moreover, it is evident that a people as primitive as the miners of Wangara would readily exchange their gold dust for the manufactured goods offered by the Arab merchants, or for the rock salt of the

[1] See J. J. Scarisbrick and P. L. Carter, 'An Expedition to Wangara', *Ghana Notes and Queries*, No 1 (1961).

Sahara. Indeed, before the mines were over-exploited, there was so much gold about in the Western Sudan that it was no more valuable than its weight in salt; and having no use for the metal, the kings of Ghana covered their horses and dogs with gold trappings. When Mansa Musa, the king of Mali, set out on his pilgrimage to Mecca in 1324, his caravan included 100 camels carrying between them some thirteen and a half tons of gold, which the monarch gave away as other men dispersed copper coins. It seemed self-evident to Europeans who heard of these African kings that there must exist, somewhere in their territories, gold mines of incalculable wealth. The question was where? And how did one get there?

The Italians were the first and most active in attempting to solve the mystery. We have vague records of several of them— in one case of a traveller who was reputed to have crossed the Sahara with a salt caravan in 1283. Two hundred years later Antonio Malfante, a merchant of Genoa, sent back from the Tuat oasis in Algeria a secret report to his partner, Antonio Marinoni, itemizing the information he had collected about the Niger River and Timbuctoo, and warning Marinoni not to divulge these trade secrets to anyone. In the letter he regrets that he could discover nothing specific about the source of the Sudanese gold, which was the principal reason for his arduous journey:

> I frequently inquired where the gold was found and how it was collected and invariably was told by my host, 'I have lived fourteen years in the country of the Blacks, and I have never seen or heard anyone who could say with certainty, "This is what I have witnessed, this is how they find and collect the gold . . . " '[1]

---

[1] *'Interrogavi satis ubi aurum reperitur . . .'* Letter written from Tuat in 1447 by Antonio Malfante. See Charles Germain Bourel de la Roncière, *La Decouverte de l' Afrique au moyen age.* Cairo: La Société Royale de Géographie d'Egypte, 1924, Vol 5, p 151.

In 1407 yet another Italian adventurer claimed to have crossed the Sahara and to have reached Timbuctoo, this one the Florentine Benedetto Dei. But we have difficulty believing a man who boasted, among other things, that he brought back from Beirut a snake with a hundred teeth and four legs. More likely is the story of a French sailor called Paul Imbert, a slave of the Pacha Hamar, a Portuguese eunuch, who reached Timbuctoo on 27 March 1618, with 400 riflemen. Imbert went along as 'navigator', implying, presumably, that he was expected to plot a course as for ocean travel: that is, on a direct line from Marrakesh to Timbuctoo. But anybody who has travelled with a caravan in the Sahara knows that this sort of compass-and-sextant navigation is impracticable, especially in crossing sand seas where the line and condition of the dunes determine the best course. However, even if the French sailor's expertise was for all practical purposes useless on this thousand-mile crossing of the western Sahara, there is no reason to doubt that he along with a number of other Europeans in the service of Mouley Zidan, sultan of Morocco and conqueror of the Sudan, did reach Timbuctoo. A letter written in 1623 by a French merchant called Charant to a colleague in Paris states that '*Paul Imbert nous faisoit souvent reçit de son voyage de Tambouctou comme d'un voyage de grande fatigue et de grande consequence.*'[1]

We are also told that Imbert's journey took two months; that the caravan travelled only at night and carried all the provisions required by men and beasts; and that the principal item of exchange for the Sudanese gold was the rock salt of the Taodeni mines.

Gold is no longer exchanged for salt in the markets of Timbuctoo, or brought across the Sahara from the mines of Wangara to the merchant bankers of Fez and Marrakesh in Morocco. The African mines, indeed, ceased to be of importance almost overnight as the gold of Central and South America reached Europe in Spanish galleons loaded with the

[1] Bourel de la Roncière, *op cit*, pp 165–6.

booty of the Conquistadors. Prior to Columbus's discovery of the New World, European bankers and merchants had been obliged to rely on Africa and the Arabs for much of the specie needed to pay for their imports from the East Indies. But already by the middle of the sixteenth century, as a result of Columbus's expedition, the Spanish conquerors of Mexico and Peru were working the fabulously rich deposits of Central America and sending enormous quantities of gold back to Europe. And soon only a negligible amount of the precious metal was being transported from the West African mines to Morocco, and the Arabs who had preserved a monopoly of the trans-Saharan gold trade for 200 years next turned their attention to other and more profitable commodities. The Gold Road across the Great Desert now became the highway of the salt and slave caravans and the mines of Wangara a footnote of African history.

The African Caravans—Salt

The entire population of the Niger river basin has depended on the Saharan salt deposits for at least the last 2,000 years. The Sudan itself is almost totally devoid of salt, which the inhabitants require even more than those of northern climes, since the negro sweats more than the white man and hence loses his body salt more quickly. In addition, his flocks and herds need a plentiful supply of this vital ingredient in view of the poor quality of the grazing lands. So salt was for a long time worth its weight in gold on the Timbuctoo market, and the caravans transporting it have long been among the largest and most remunerative in Africa.

There are two methods of producing salt in the Sahara—by mining and by panning. The former method is used in the most famous of the mines, at the oasis of Taodeni, which has been worked since 1585 when the Moroccan sultan Muhammed deliberately destroyed the ancient salt mines at Teghaza. The slave-workers of this place were thereupon taken eastwards by the tribe that owned them to the deposits at Taodeni, which have been exploited without cessation from 1585 to the present. The yield of these mines is so lucrative that no matter what dangers and difficulties and outright sufferings are involved in exploiting the trade, there are always men who actually volunteer to work in the appalling conditions of salt-mining, and others who are prepared to cross waterless deserts as camel-drivers.

The second method of obtaining the precious substance is by panning from open pits, and it is this method which is used in the oases of the Central Sahara, notably at Bilma in the Republic of Niger. It was Bilma and the neighbouring oasis of Fachi which supplied, and still supplies, the populous Hausa country with a very fine grade of salt in return for which the whole chain of oases along the Kawar depression receives supplies of grain and other essentials from the outside world. And this trade, wholly dependent upon salt, employed tens of thousands of men and camels which formed the bi-annual *azalais* which crossed the dreaded Ténéré sand sea and can still be seen crossing it today.

The richest and at the same time the most dreadful of the Saharan deposits was, and continues to be, Taodeni in Mali, which in a good year yields 2,000 tons of rock salt dug out in the form of rectangular slabs, each of which weighs about thirty kilos. These slabs, four to six of which are loaded on a camel, resemble blocks of grey concrete and are almost as hard. In fact, the Taodeni salt is quarried very much like anthracite coal; for like coal, it is found underground in seams.

The extraordinary thing about the salt mines of the Sahara is that the methods of working them and the life of the miners have not changed in a thousand years, for the descriptions by the first Arab travellers coincide exactly with what the visitor sees today. This is how the fourteenth-century historian, Ibn Battuta, describes one of the mines he visited:

> an unattractive Village, with the curious feature that its houses and mosques are built of salt. There are no trees there, nothing but sand. In the sand is a salt mine. They dig for the salt, and find it in thick slabs. . . .[1]

Conditions at the mines are no better today—no better, because no different. Imagine a community in the middle of a desert, distinguishable only by a row of hovels roughly built

[1] Ibn Battuta, *Travels in Asia and Africa*, translated by H. A. R. Gibb. London, 1929, p 317–318.

out of blocks of salt: such is the mine of Taodeni, and here live the black miners throughout the two to five years of their contract. They number about 100, some known as 'prisoners'—that is, forced labourers; others called 'freemen', otherwise debtors. All of them work seven days a week, two or three days being set aside for the payment of debts in the case of the 'freemen'. The salt is hacked out with hoes and pick-axes from the clay which encloses it, either at the bottom of shafts or in the galleries where miners follow a vein of salt exactly as they do in a coal or tin mine. The workman has to squat or lie down in the galleries, or to stand in the brine that collects at the bottom of the shafts. Eventually he will be covered with sores which eat away his flesh. His diet consists of dried foods and preserves, and the least delay in the bi-annual food convoy from Timbuctoo might mean death by starvation. In 1910, fifty-six men, or over half the population of the mines, died in this way.

The cost in suffering of getting this salt out of the ground and of transporting it to Timbuctoo is, of course, enormous: the life expectancy of a miner at Taodeni is two to three years; of a camel hard-worked on the trail, six to seven years—whereas, well treated, a camel will work for twenty years. In addition, the loss of camels through exhaustion is liable to be as high as one out of ten, though the death of these animals in the desert is not regarded as an unmitigated misfortune, since the water in its stomach will be saved, and the flesh will be eaten by men whose diet is woefully deficient in protein.

Bilma in contrast to Taodeni is more fortunate and remains to this day a busy and thriving community, even if it is one of the most isolated places in the world. Happily for the natives, who almost without exception are engaged in the exploitation of the salt pans, the business of extracting the product is much easier than it is in Taodeni. The villagers leave their houses in the early morning and walk or ride their donkeys across the plain to the hills and ridges which are composed of rock salt. Here they hack out pits of about three metres square and two metres deep. These pits quickly fill with salt water which percolates up through the hillocks. Evaporation causes a crust to form on the surface. The crust is continually broken, the salt mush sinks to the bottom of the pool and there crystallizes. The finished salt is then scooped out of the pit and poured into moulds made from the boles of palm trees. When the salt has set in the form of round or conical 'loaves', it is removed from the mould and piled up to await the camels which will transport it across the Ténéré to Agadez.

The actual production of the salt goes on during the period of most intense heat and evaporation—from April to October. There will then be hundreds of pits at work, attended by everybody of working age in Bilma, including the small children. Each person, man, woman, and child, has his special function. The mines, in general, belong to the whole community, but are administered by the chief men of the village, who alone can authorize the digging of new pits. The salt of Bilma and Fachi, the other oasis, is slightly inferior to that of Taodeni, but its two productions, *beza* for human consumption and *kantou* for animals, are of enormous commercial value, which explains why the Tuareg, those former brigands of the desert, have always protected the people and deposits of Bilma.

Desert people and the inhabitants of the central Sudan (Mali, the Republic of Niger, Upper Volta) prefer rock salt to the Western variety—not only prefer it, but seem to crave it, as many Westerners crave sweet foods. One sees the slabs and bars and cones of this mineral salt in every town and village along the Niger river, waiting to be transported inland by camel. Salt, in fact, is the equivalent of hard money; and everybody who is involved in its production, exportation, and transport can count himself well off.

It is the Tuareg, the famous Veiled Men, who in February and October organize the bi-annual salt caravans one of

The author examines rock paintings left by prehistoric inhabitants of the Central Sahara. *Below*: Arab fort at Mourzouk, capital of the Fezzan and once an important station on the trans-Saharan slave route

A Tuareg camel-man spends an entire day at a desert well watering his herd. *Below*: The salt pits at Bilma which supply nearly the whole of the southern Sahara with this vital commodity

which in 1913 actually numbered 25,000 camels. These *azalai* march for five days across a desert without a single well or blade of grass. On the outward journey, when the animals carry bags of millet, rice, and the other necessities (and a few luxuries) for the oases at Bilma and Fachi, some camels disappear completely under veritable haystacks, which are to be the fodder en route. If well fed and watered before setting out, the healthy and strong camels will survive the journey without drinking, though five days will be the limit of their endurance. How much endurance is needed for both men and beasts who have to march fifteen hours a day is seen from the sun-bleached skeletons which mark the trail as clearly as beacons all the way from the Arbre du Ténéré well—a well with a single tree which finally collapsed and died in 1975— to the outskirts of Fachi. The arrival of the *azalai*—3,000 camels strung out in parallel columns as far as the eye can see—is one of the great sights of the world.

On arrival in the oasis, the camel-men are welcomed as the victors of a great battle. Each of them is more or less bound by custom and service to a particular family, and it will be the salt produced by this family that he will buy and transport to the market. He will pay in needed supplies—millet, rice, tea, and sugar. The villagers produce nearly all their other basic foods such as vegetables, fruit, and meat. Nowadays, of course, their tastes are more sophisticated, and it is not impossible after the caravans have arrived with the goods to obtain whisky, beer, Coca-cola, and cigarettes in the little shops. The French army always had a detachment of either the Foreign Legion or of colonial troops stationed here in the forts at Bilma, Fachi, and the other oases strung out along the main north-south highway between the Fezzan and the Chad, so that the nomads soon became accustomed to the ways of Europeans. The French, however, or more especially those of them who regarded themselves as true *Sahariens* in the tradition of General Laperrine of the Camel Corps and

7

Father de Foucauld, missionary to the Tuareg, always sought to keep the desert untainted by Western ideas and practices, and it was largely because of their attitude that the salt caravans on which the entire economy of the nomads now depends have survived. For it is not just the families at Bilma who are involved in the salt-trade—the nomads of the region for hundreds of miles around depend for their livelihood on the transport of salt. Camels are bred for this purpose; men are trained to cross the desert as guides or camel-drivers; boys are reared to watch the herds in their summer pastures; women and girls are employed in the oasis gardens to grow millet and food for the caravaners; and so on.

However, as the Saharan states with their new independence and eagerness to belong to the modern industrial world compare the standard of living of the oasis-dwellers with with those of city-dwellers in the West, they will decide that the camel is as obsolete as the chariot; and those progressive politicians educated at the London School of Economics will automatically equate the old ways of the desert with colonialism.

But there are other forces at work throughout the Sahara and the neighbouring states about which Western politicians, experts, and commentators who have never lived in the desert know nothing. The most powerful and insidious of these is the ancient hostility between the Berbers and the negroes, which is another facet of the hostility between whites and blacks in general. In short, Berbers who are all Moslems and, for the most part, Arabic-speaking have regarded themselves, and behaved, as a superior race for over a thousand years, continually raiding the black men's villages, enslaving them by the tens of thousands, and treating them as non-human. 'Allah has created negroes to be slaves, as he has made their skins black, and you can change one as little as the other,' stated a Libyan sheik to a British consul as late as 1910; and this claim typifies the general attitude of the Berber population of North Africa and the Sahara. But with the independence of the negro states south of the Sahara—Mali, Niger, Chad, and the new territories of central and eastern Africa—the old resentments and hatreds became sharper, and old scores were now able to be paid off, though none of this was official policy of the governments concerned, and none of it was really comprehended by Western politicians who make pronouncements about African affairs. But the people on the spot know what is involved: in the case of the Tuareg, for instance, it is revenge. From the point of view of the Soninke, Mandingo, Bambara, Hausa, Fulani, Beriberi, and other black tribes (many of them still pagan, though they will naturally avoid recording this on official questionnaires) the day has passed when the Tuareg warriors wantonly looted their towns, villages, and homesteads or swaggered through the markets with their great swords and their eyes glinting above the *litham* (the face cloth), so that the merchants and shopkeepers were afraid to refuse them anything they demanded.

In the old days, the black populations along the Niger were wholly dependent for their essential supplies (notably salt) on the caravans organized by the Tuareg and, further to the west towards Mauretania, by comparable camel-riding nomads like the Berabiche and Kounta. But no longer so. Today trucks and aeroplanes supply the growing cities with all the goods produced in Europe, including luxuries like frozen strawberries and necessities like salt. The camel-men and their camels are less and less needed, so they have less and less opportunity to lord it over the black Africans. The blacks now have their Mercedes cars, faster, more expensive, and more prestigious than a beautiful fawn-coloured *mehari* with the longest pedigree in the Sahara.

And when prolonged droughts and eventual famine strike this whole region, the food sent in by outside agencies is in the control of the black government officials, so it is the turn of the once all-powerful camel-riders to come begging for help. Their flocks and herds are depleted; their women and children are starving. Nomads, who once scorned those who lived in houses as people who had forfeited their freedom, are rounded up and kept behind wire on the outskirts of towns in Mali and Niger. They no longer play a vital role in the economy of the desert and the Niger river, for if they refuse to bring the salt across the sand seas on the backs of their camels, an appeal to a friendly country, usually a Communist one, will procure them all the packaged salt they need in return for a few concessions.

Discouraged and aware that their day as 'lords of the desert' is over, the nomads are less and less inclined to cross a desert like the Ténéré or make the twenty-day march across the Tanezrouft to Taodeni. When the French were the rulers of the Sahara, the Bilma salt caravan consisted of 25,000 camels and close on 1,000 men. Today 500 animals and twenty men follow the trail of carcases to the wells at the Arbre du Ténéré. An era is ending in the Sahara as surely and as quickly as it is ending in the West, and when the last salt caravan sets out for the mines at Taodeni or the salt pans of Bilma, that era will be gone for ever.

The African Caravans—Slaves

The African slave trade had been organized and developed by the Arab merchants who first penetrated into the negro kingdoms and persuaded the black rulers to spare some of the prisoners of war who were slain in the normal course of affairs —not only the old men and women, but men in the prime of life. The only useful prisoners to the negro kings were the young girls and a few young men, the former to serve as concubines, the latter as eunuchs. All the others were a mere embarrassment, needing to be fed, housed, and guarded. But the Arabs knew that a healthy man of any age up to forty, if of good physique, could still be a useful slave in the civilized world to the north, for such men were needed as labourers, porters, galley oarsmen, gardeners, and so forth. Consequently thousands of lives were saved, thanks to the more sophisticated attitude towards slavery of the Arabs, though whether the men and women who were driven across the desert to the cities of North Africa and the Middle East considered themselves better off as live slaves than as dead freemen is a matter for speculation.

But the Arab traders were not interested in saving lives for their own sake, or in questions of morality, since Islam had given religious sanction to the institution of slavery, particularly in the case of pagans. The negroes belonged to this class and were, in consequence, considered scarcely human on account of their appearance and their customs. They were known as *Lemlem*, meaning savages, and some of them were definitely cannibals. Ibn Battuta, the fourteenth-century Arab traveller, states that the Sultan of Niani received some visitors from the nearby state of Wangara with the gift of a negress whom his guests ate that evening for their supper and that this procedure did not appear to surprise anyone. Ibn Battuta also indicates the Arab disapproval of the blacks by drawing attention to the way in which women, including the sultan's daughters, walked around without a stitch of clothing to cover them, though this custom, he says, was not surprising with a people who ate the flesh of dogs and donkeys. All in all, the supercilious and fastidious Arab did not regard the negro as a fellow-human, and he had no more moral compunction about enslaving him than he would have had of putting an ox to the plough.

All over Africa the slave caravaners were on the move right up to, and into, the twentieth century, creating a network of trails that covered the entire northern half of the continent and bringing a period of great desolation to the central kingdoms; for by the seventeenth century Africa was providing the Christian as well as the Moslem world with hundreds of thousands of slaves a year. By then there were two separate trade routes: that of the Europeans centred on the West African coast from whose ports the slave ships took out an estimated 14,000,000 men, women, and children between 1550 and 1850; and that of the Arabs whose principal markets were located along the North African littoral and handled an estimated 10,000 slaves a year.

The busiest Arab slave route was the trans-Saharan trail which ran up from Lake Chad via the Tibesti to Mourzouk in the Fezzan, where the captives, exhausted and emaciated by their long journey, were rested and fattened up before being sent north again to the market at Tripoli. It is a strange feeling even today to stand inside the old Arab fort at Mourzouk where the newly arrived slaves were passed through the Turkish customs: one or two of the more attractive of the women would be sent along to the nearby fort, now a jumble of ruins, as a present for the commandant. Then, as soon as the remainder had rested after their long journey, off they went again across the Fezzan by the same road that had been travelled since Carthaginian times, the Way of the Garamantes.

The extent of the slave trade, in the absence of precise records, can be roughly estimated from the report of the French explorer Henri Duveyrier, who reached Mourzouk in 1860. In that year, he says, captive negroes were passing through the Fezzanese capital at the rate of 2,000 to 3,000 per annum, this number being approximately fifty per cent of the 5,000 who had set out from Kano, the remainder having died *en route*. Assuming, then, that 5,000 slaves a year were sent north from the Chad region, the total during the eighteenth and nineteenth centuries, when the trade was at its most active, would mean the dispatch of something like a million along this one route alone, if Duveyrier's estimate was correct.

The slave trade was so profitable that a young 'trained' negro, according to Ibn Battuta, was worth several camels, and camels were always symbolic of wealth in the Sahara. Two centuries after Battuta, the Moorish geographer al-Hassan ibn Muhammad al-Wazzani, better known as Leo Africanus, protégé of Pope Leo X, listed the going price for slaves in the Barbary market as: a male slave, twenty ducats; a female, thirty; and a eunuch, fifty.[1] And since Leo states that slaves were now cheaper than camels, which were selling at fifty ducats each, and a great deal cheaper than civet cats (200 ducats), it is clear that the consignments coming up the Slave Road were growing ever larger and more frequent. Mourzouk, the staging post where the exhausted captives were rested before proceeding to the northern markets, had, in consequence, become one of the richest towns in Africa.

Mourzouk today is not much different in appearance from

---

[1] Two Venetian ducats were worth roughly a gold sovereign. The value of a gold sovereign fluctuates so widely that it is futile to try and translate these sums into present-day currencies.

the time when Friedrich Hornemann presented himself to the Sultan Muhammed-ben Sultan Mansur in the vice-regal palace on 20 January 1798. The Sultan has gone, but the palace remains—a jumble of toppled stones and mud bricks, extensive and ramshackle in typical Turkish style, though once regarded by Turks and locals as a luxurious and elegant mansion. Here Hornemann saw Muhammed 'seated on an old-fashioned elbow chair, apparelled in a large white frock or shirt, brocaded with silver and gold; but the most remarkable appearance is that of his turban which from the fore to the hinder part extends a full yard and is not less than two-thirds of a yard in breadth.'[1] This, then, was the Sultan of Fezzan in the year 1798, a prince of sorts who lived in the palace at Mourzouk with the sultana, his eunuchs, and some forty concubines who were changed as often as the slave caravans arrived.

Some hundred years later another foreigner in the service of the British reached Mourzouk; and so slowly did things change in the Sahara that the Swiss Hanns Vischer, MA, FRGS, proceeding south to Bornu by the old slave route, found the oasis town of Mourzouk much as it was in Hornemann's day. He had travelled with almost the last caravan of its kind the world would ever see, a caravan which was typical of a thousand years of Saharan history.[2] His fellow-travellers were Mecca pilgrims returning to their homes in Northern Nigeria; liberated slaves from Libya and Tunisia; Tibbu and Arab camel-drivers who had brought a northbound caravan from Lake Chad to Tripoli and now wished to return; merchants with their wares; and discharged soldiers. Its departure from Tripoli was typical: the camels were loaded up at first light and by 10 o'clock the same morning the entire cargo had been dumped by the bolting animals for several miles along the

---

[1] *Missions to the Niger. The Journal of Friedrich Hornemann's Travels 1797–1798*, ed. by E. W. Bovill. Cambridge: University Press, 1964, pp 101, 102.
[2] Hanns Vischer, *Across the Sahara*. London: Arnold, 1910.

trail. The *azalai* finally got away late in the afternoon. Typical, too, was the hostility of the sheiks and holy men through whose country the British consul had to pass. They stated outright that they distrusted all Christians because such infidels would contaminate their lands, steal their country, ruin their trade, and even try to persuade their brother Moslems to abandon the true faith.

Vischer arrived in Mourzouk on 22 August 1908 and realized, as every traveller who stands in its dilapidated market place must, that here was a town once as famous in Africa as Algiers is today. For almost every great Libyan explorer of the nineteenth century passed through Mourzouk on his way to the Chad, Niger, and West Africa. A number of the first are buried here or hereabouts: Hornemann's companion, Joseph Frendenburgh in 1799; Joseph Ritchie in 1820; and Alexandrine Tinne in 1869. Indeed, the people of the town were still talking about the Danish woman-explorer as the 'king's daughter', when Vischer arrived with his caravan forty years later, for her murder by the Tuareg was one of the most sensational in the long history of the Slave Road.

The old capital of the Fezzan had already lost all semblance of its wealth and importance by the beginning of this century when the slave trade was ending and the caravans were taking other and less dangerous routes. The town no longer had any special reason to exist, except as a place of exile for political prisoners—in other words, educated, liberal-minded men who had become a nuisance to the Turkish authorities. The British consul met Turks who were jailed in the old dungeon one day and released to be secretary to the Governor the next—men who spoke several languages and quoted Hegel, Kant, Omar Khayyam, and the Arab classics with equal facility.

Hanns Vischer saw only the vestiges of the slave caravans which came up from the Chad: the earlier African travellers saw the real thing, since they were often obliged to travel with the slaves. One of the first of these explorers was James Richardson

(1806–1851) who made a special study of the trans-Saharan slave traffic. On 23 March 1850 he left Tripoli with two German scientists, Heinrich Barth and Adolf Overweg, the former of whom was to become the greatest of all African explorers, while the latter, also an explorer of the first rank, was, like Richardson himself, to die on this long journey. The three men travelled together as far as the Air Mountains, then separated to explore Lake Chad individually. It was from this area that thousands of slaves were taken by the *razzias*, or Arab raids on native villages. The traders had their merchandise strictly classified and price-listed, as Richardson discovered in Zinder. He classifies the captives in descending order of their value as follows:

Males	*Females*
1. Boys without beards	1. Girls with little breasts
2. Those with beard beginning	2. Those with breasts plump
3. Grown boys	3. Thin girls
4. Adolescent boys	4. Adolescent girls
5. Men with a beard	5. Women with breasts hanging down

According to Richardson, it was the negro kings who supplied the majority of the victims to the Arab merchants, while 'the blacks themselves can see their neighbours torn away from their houses and carried off in irons with the greatest indifference.'[1]

I passed the slave-market (he writes), and was greatly shocked to see a poor old woman for sale amongst the rest of the human beings. She was offered for about six thousand *wadas*, or about ten shillings in English money. It is quite

[1] James Richardson, *Narrative of a Mission to Central Africa*. London: Murray, 1853, p 236.

impossible to conjecture of what use such a poor old creature could be.[1]

It is not, therefore, surprising that the slaves destined for the Mediterranean markets should receive no better treatment than the camels and donkeys that formed the caravan. What that treatment was we know from a detailed report by an early African explorer who travelled the Slave Road from Mourzouk to Tripoli. This was George Francis Lyon, Royal Navy captain, who accomplished more original and varied exploration in his short lifetime—he died aged thirty-seven—than many Victorian travellers who achieved greater fame. Captain Lyon's work in the Arctic region and Hudson Bay does not concern us here, except to note the remarkable versatility of a man who could be marching with a caravan in Libya when the temperature was 133°F in the shade in June 1820, and wintering in the Arctic a year later. Four years after his journey to the Arctic, he was exploring the interior of Mexico, and after Mexico, Brazil. He died on his way back to England in 1832, for like all the other African explorers, with the exception of Heinrich Barth, his health had been so weakened by what was then called 'the fever' that he was destined to die young.

But his book, *A Narrative of Travels in Northern Africa in the Years 1818, 19 and 20*[2], is as fresh today as it was when first published. For the interior of the Fezzan and the oases which lie along the old caravan routes have not changed all that much, despite the coming and going of the diesel trucks which have replaced the camels. Captain Lyon, moreover, is an excellent companion, for his bluff sailor's attitude towards the world is in sharp contrast to the mealy-mouthed view of the Victorian missionaries who were to follow the explorers down the trails into Black Africa. His description of the modes

[1] *Op cit*, p 230.
[2] London: Murray, 1821.

and manners of the North Africans is not meant to spare the
sensibilities or blushes of his readers in the comfort of their
drawing-rooms. He informs us that the prostitutes of Tripoli,
who were very numerous, 'were obliged daily to supply food
for the Bashaw's dogs'—a curious custom inspiring one to
wonder why; that Moors were never employed as hangmen,
'but the first Jew who happens to be at hand has that office
conferred upon him'; that thieves had their hands cut off, the
operation being performed with a razor; and that eructation
was performed as often and loudly as possible.

> Great men go through this ceremony with a solemnity and
> dignity altogether imposing; striking their beards and thank-
> ing God for the great relief they have obtained.

Even young lads of eight years, Lyon adds, 'promised fair to
become quite professors in the art.'[1]

As for the ladies, the gallant captain had an appreciative eye,
noting what pretty eyes and names they had. One of the
bashaw's wives was called Zaitoon, meaning 'Olive Tree';
another, Zeman Donya, or 'Time of the World'. Lilla Fatma,
the wife of Sheikh Barood, on the other hand, was remarkable
as being, in the eyes of the Libyans, the most beautiful woman
in the world. Lyon's description of her is a gem of early
travel writing.

> On my entrance she veiled herself as to exhibit to advantage
> her arm, with all its gay ornaments; and on my requesting
> to be favoured with a view of her face, she, with very little
> reluctance, gratified me. Her chin, the tip of her nose, and
> the space between her eyebrows, were marked with black
> lines; she was much rouged; her neck, arms, and legs were
> covered with tattooed flowers, open hands, circles, the
> names of God, and of her numerous male friends. She had

---

[1] *Op cit*, p 14.

a multitude of gold ear-rings and ornaments, set with very bad and counterfeit jewels, and weighing altogether, I should think, two or three pounds. Her shirt was of striped silk; and she had a rich purple silk barracan, or mantle, gracefully thrown round her and fastened at the breast by a gold pin, with ornaments of the same metal suspended from it: all the other articles of finery which she possessed were displayed round the tent, whilst a multitude of poor thin wretches, resembling witches, sat round her in astonishment, never in their lives having seen such a paragon of perfection. Like all other Arabs, they touched whatever pleased them most, one admiring this object, another something near it, so that our poor belle was poked by a dozen fingers at once; all, however, agreeing on one point, that she was beautifully and excessively fat, and I must say I never before beheld such a monstrous mass of human flesh. One of her legs, of enormous size, was uncovered as high as the calf, and everyone pressed it, admiring its solidity and praising God for blessing them with such a sight. I was received most graciously and invited to sit close to her.[1]

What a picture the sailor presents for us, and what an amusing companion he must have been. His actual fellow-traveller, Mr Joseph Ritchie, was a much more sober character, who, upon entering Lilla's tent, caused all singing and dancing to stop abruptly.

But the captain was to see and describe less pleasing sights than Lilla, the fat wife of Sheikh Barood. On 9 February 1820, the temperature being 1°30 below zero, Lyon left Mourzouk bound for Tripoli with a slave caravan. The Englishman's group consisted of his servant, a sailor called Bedford, four Arab attendants, eight pack-camels, two trotting camels, two sheep, and a horse. The road north of Mourzouk crosses an empty desert and being so exposed is particularly cold and

[1] *Op cit*, pp 62–3.

uncomfortable in February, which is the month of winds. The slave-traders, aware that cold in the desert can kill just as certainly as thirst, had clad their female slaves in warm clothes. The girls were also issued green or yellow caps with large flaps for the ears. Both sexes were given sandals, as they had to walk some 500 miles to market. The girls marched separately from the men, who followed the camel-train. At 1 o'clock, the slaves were watered along with the animals that needed water (not the camels). Like the sheep and goats, the slaves were made to drink from large bowls placed on the ground. Having been watered, off they marched again in their platoons. Tiny children who could not keep up were simply tossed on to the back of a camel. Those over six years of age were forced to keep trotting on, sometimes for fourteen or fifteen hours a day. As always in the desert, the duration of the day's march was rigorously determined by the distance between wells. There could be no arguments or compromises about this: the law of the desert applies to sultan and slave alike.

For food, the slaves were given a quart of dates in the morning, which had to last them until the evening meal. Dates, of course, are the most nourishing of foods in the desert, and it was quite customary for camel riders to travel for many days with nothing more to eat than a small sack of dates and a goatskin of water. In the evening when the caravan stopped, a porridge was made of millet. This was served into a bowl, a hole was made in the centre with a stick, and sometimes gravy or butter was poured into the cavity. When supper had been eaten, the women slaves lay down in one line, the men in another well separated from them, and all were covered over with sacking until morning.

During the night any of the masters or camel-drivers who desired a sleeping partner chose a girl or a boy from the company, making exceptions of those girls who were known to be virgins. These girl-children, as valuable merchandise, were carefully guarded.

A journey with a caravan is, under the best of conditions, a terrible physical and mental ordeal which becomes unbearable if one of the company, no matter who he is, whether free or slave, rich or poor, falls sick. There is very little that can be done, since the caravan cannot stop, and there is seldom sufficient room on any of the camels to enable the sufferer to be carried. The camels are always loaded to the limit of their strength with vital supplies, especially water. Consequently if any of the slaves fell behind out of weakness, fatigue, or sickness (dysentery and typhoid were the principal diseases), they would either be left to die of hunger, cold, and thirst; or be driven along by the threats and sometimes the whips of the merchants. Western observers like Captain Lyon were, of course, appalled by such treatment, but in fact the caravaners had no alternative. As they did not want to lose their merchandise, if a slave was really so ill that she could not walk and no amount of shouting and striking could get her on her feet again, she was sometimes thrown over the back of a camel and carried to the next camp-site where her companions did what they could for her. But there were no medicines whatsoever available; if the sick person died, a shallow grave was dug by the other slaves, and the caravan moved on.

In this matter of endurance, Lyon makes the interesting observation that the female slaves were much less exhausted by the long marches (sometimes thirty miles in a day) than the men; and even more interesting, he points out that the girls always marched as a little band, singing in chorus, encouraging the unhappy, and helping the weary. Most extraordinary of all was the gaiety of the very little children who were continually playing and chasing each other even on the march, so that, like dogs out for a walk, they must have covered at least twice the ground traversed by the adults. Four little girls from the ages of four to eight, whom one of the slave-dealers had acquired in the Chad, played in this manner all the way to Tripoli. In fact, the four-year-old was

still dancing and jumping about when the grown-up slaves
had fallen exhausted into their first sleep, so that she actually
became something of a pest to her companions.

A slave caravan, at least on this Chad-Tripoli route, was
therefore not the horrible and brutal spectacle that one would
have expected it to be. Those who have crossed a desert
with a caravan know that there is really no need and no room
for unkindness, let alone cruelty, towards one's fellow-
travellers. The problem of endurance surpasses everything:
one has no energy left for open quarrels. At the same time,
the almost continual danger and the continuous discomfort in
surroundings so formidable and mysterious as the desert
eventually weld the caravaners into a sort of family. There
are even many moments of extreme happiness and gaiety, as
when a splendid camp-site with plenty of pasture for the
camels has been found, a gazelle has been killed and roasted,
a large fire throws its ruddy light over the travellers sprawled
on the ground, and somebody starts singing.

Even Captain Lyon, who was exhausted and sick as he
accompanied the caravan up the Slave Road, had these
moments of supreme pleasure, particularly on watching the
black girls dance and listening to them singing. The fact was
that these girls, so gallant and so full of the joy of living, were
incapable of being depressed and miserable. They knew, of
course, that they were slaves and were destined for a concubine's role in some Turkish or Tunisian harem; but we should
not suppose that this fate was as awful to them as it would
have seemed to Victorian abolitionists. John Lewis
Burckhardt, the explorer of Nubia and Arabia and an authority
from first-hand study of slavery, is positive on this point,
though in no sense condoning the infamous trade or, in
particular, 'the vile traders':

The treatment which the slaves experience from the traders
[he writes] is rather kind than otherwise. The slaves are

A warrior of the Tuareg, or People of the Veil, once the Lords of the Great Desert

The mosque of Timbuctoo, the legendary city famous for its wealth and learning

A slave caravan as depicted by Captain George Francis Lyon, RN, who accompanied the 'kaffle' from Mourzouk to Tripoli in 1820

generally taught to call their masters Abouy (my father) and to consider themselves as their children. They are seldom flogged, are well fed, are not over-worked, and are spoken to in a kind manner . . . [On the road] the health of the slave is always attended to: he is regularly fed, and receives his share of water at the same time that his master drinks; and the youngest and most delicate of the females are permitted to ride on the camels.[1]

In other words, the traders treated their stock like cattle were treated in Western countries: the market value of a bull or cow obviously depended upon its physical well-being. And the Arab slave-traders were at least not directly guilty of the most infamous cruelty of all: the mutilation of boys intended for the harem. Castration was performed either by negro operators back in the villages, or, in the case of the Egyptian trade, by Coptic priests, two of whom ran what Burckhardt calls a 'manufactory' at their village near Siout in Upper Egypt. The explorer describes the priests' method of operation for those who know Latin and care to read about how it was performed; and he adds:

The operation is always performed upon the strongest and best-looking boys; but it has a visible effect upon their features when they arrive at full age. The faces of the eunuchs whom I saw in the Hedjaz appeared almost destitute of flesh, the eye hollow, the cheek bones prominent, and the whole physiognomy having a skeleton-like appearance by which the eunuch may generally be recognized at first sight.[2]

The eunuch's appearance is hardly surprising inasmuch as the castration entailed the total excision of the genitalia and was

[1] John Lewis Burckhardt, *Travels in Egypt and Nubia*, Second Edition. London: John Murray, 1822, pp 297, 298.
[2] *Op cit*, p 295.
8

performed by the negro operators with a sharp flint, and by the Coptic priests with a razor, in both cases without benefit of anaesthesia.

Some 5,000 slaves a year were brought out of central Africa by the great east-west caravan highway from Timbuctoo to Shendi on the Blue Nile, Shendi once being the principal market-town of the Egyptian Sudan. The lucky ones were bought by humane masters, in which case the males were treated like children of the family, according to Burckhardt, though the females did not fare so well on account of the jealousy of their mistresses. 'Slavery in the East has little dreadful in it but name,' he concludes, remarking that once the enslaved negroes had outgrown their fear of being *eaten* by white people and of becoming lousy with fleas, which were at this time unknown in the interior of Africa, they were reasonably well-off thanks to their 'propensity to mirth and frolic'.

Captain Lyon comes to much the same conclusion as Burckhardt, though the trans-Saharan route that the naval officer took from Mourzouk to Tripoli was more severe than the east-west highway which ran south of the actual desert. Nevertheless, Lyon, as we have seen, remarks on the cheerfulness of the slaves, or, more particularly, of the young negresses who evidently enjoyed their journey provided they did not fall sick and who looked forward to more adventure at the end of it. But the men, he says, walked alone, wrapped in their own misery. The reason is that they were destined for the mines and quarries, or worse, for the galleys. The girls who finished up in a large and well-organized seraglio could certainly consider themselves better off than their sisters who lived a serf-like existence in their native village. And any girl who was beautiful and lucky enough to become a great man's favourite would be treated like a veritable sultana. Not a few slave-concubines rose to positions of power in the Moslem world.

But whatever the reason for their cheerfulness, the girls who travelled with Lyon took great pains to remain feminine and attractive—'their love of finery never ceasing, even when no one was near to admire them':

> Though overcome by privation of every kind and by the fatigue of a long day's journey, they employed themselves in converting into neck ornaments, snail shells, berries, or any other whimsical objects they could meet with. Those who possessed rings, bead bands for the head, or silver ear-rings never failed to put them on when they stopped for the night, washing and oiling their skins whenever they had an opportunity. They also constantly used kohl to blacken their eyelids and to make different marks on the face.[1]

The kind and humane captain, who had done everything he could to help the slaves, even walking himself, though suffering from dysentery, in order that a sick girl might be carried on his horse, parted from his travelling companions with real regret.

> Their good-humoured gaiety and songs had lightened to me many hours of pain and fatigue, and their gratitude for any little benefits I had it in my power to confer had quite warmed my heart towards them. Even when so exhausted as to be almost unable to walk, these poor creatures showed few instances of sulkiness and despondency: the first stanza of a song having been sung by one, immediately the whole caravan joined in the chorus.[2]

'These poor creatures' had walked nearly 2,000 miles when they arrived at Tripoli, still singing. Some of the smallest had been born on the road and had survived even when the mother had no milk. Lyon reports such a case of 'a little male child

[1] *Op cit*, p 341.
[2] *Op cit*, p 341.

which was carried in turns by the whole kaffle'. The baby was fed on a mixture of cold water and flour and lived. Indeed, a great many of these cheerful and innocent creatures, driven across the sands under the burning sun, survived because of the love they gave each other. Lyon, too, was sustained by this spirit and so completed his journey. Characteristic of the early explorers of the Sahara, he apologizes for having 'omitted to notice the variations of the Thermometer from the 28th of February to the present time, 25th March 1820.' We do not mind his omission of temperature readings and are grateful for his description of that little black girl who was still dancing when the long day's march was done.

Timbuctoo and the Way Thither

The main terminus of the African caravan system was Timbuctoo. Situated where one of the three great African rivers meets the Great Desert, Timbuctoo became not only a major commercial centre, but a crucible of the Arab-African races, religions, and cultures. Yet for centuries it remained a complete mystery to Europeans, a magic name familiar to people who had never heard of Cairo, Damascus, or Peking. It was the dream of all nineteenth-century explorers to reach this fabulous terminus of the caravans.

The fascination that this African town originally held for the Western world, however, was due to the same kind of illusion that made Eldorado irresistible to the Conquistadors: the craze to discover a country fabulously rich in gold. And just as the exploration of Central and South America was mainly the result of Spanish adventurers searching for the capitals of a mythical Eldorado, so the early exploration of the Sahara was due to the efforts of British, French, and German travellers to reach Timbuctoo and the Niger river. The importance of their ventures both to the scientific as well as the commercial world is reflected in the valuable prizes offered by the British and the French to the first man to reach Timbuctoo and return with a description of that city: the British prize was worth £2,500; the French, 7,000 francs, a gold medal, and a pension. In addition, the first explorer to reach Timbuctoo and to live to tell the tale was assured of international fame and fortune. In these circumstances, men were quite prepared to die on this most dangerous assignment and many of them did. Between 1789 and 1889—that is, during the first hundred years of Saharan exploration—165 explorers and travellers died of disease or were murdered in the Great Desert. They included *all* of the first seven explorers commissioned by the African Society to cross the Sahara.

But it was now imperative in the interest of trade, as well as geography, to discover the location of those negro kingdoms which used Timbuctoo as the clearing house for their gold, ivory, and slaves. Where were the countries called by the Arabs Bornu, Hausa, Fulani, Wangara, and so on? The assumption was that once an explorer could reach Timbuctoo, the mystery as to the whereabouts of these black kingdoms would be solved, their kings would accept diplomatic relations with the European princes, and their well-hidden gold mines would be available for exploitation.

Europeans had, of course, known for centuries the link between Timbuctoo, the gold mines of the negro kingdoms, and the caravan trade which enriched the world of Islam. The belief that the wealth of negroland was incalculable had been largely promulgated by the legends which had sprung up around the figure of Mansa Musa, the fourteenth-century emperor of Mali, a monarch once as celebrated in Europe as Prester John, with whom he was sometimes confused. On the other hand, a considerable core of hard facts was available concerning the African kingdoms, thanks to the Arab historians and geographers who had crossed the Sahara and visited the countries of the Niger basin as early as the tenth century. An Arab of Baghdad, Ibn Haukal, for instance, gave an account of the Western Sudan through which he travelled in AD 950—reporting, incidentally, that the Niger flowed east-wards, a statement that was contradicted two centuries later by another Arab geographer, al-Idrisi, who maintained that it flowed to the *west*. Two hundred years later again—that is, in the fourteenth century—the respected Ibn Battuta declared that he had *seen* the river flowing to the east, only to be gainsaid by the most famous of all the Arab travellers, Leo Africanus, who claimed that he had travelled *with* the current of the river in a westerly direction. It was little wonder that European geographers almost gave up hope of producing even a rough and ready atlas of central Africa, which explains Swift's characteristic jingle:

Geographers in Afric-maps,
With savage pictures fill their gaps;
And o'er unhabitable downs
Place elephants for want of towns.

Yet there was no 'want of towns' in Leo the African's *History and Description of Africa*. His accounts of Sijilmassa, Tlemcen, Wargla, Ghadames, Timbuctoo, Mali, Jenne, Gao, and many other communities were interesting to scholars, but of no practical use to the European merchants who were primarily interested in the gold that Leo was always referring to—'the plates and sceptres of gold, some of which weigh 1,300 pounds, belonging to the rich king of Timbuctoo.' And what business-men wanted to find out was the caravan trail along which the trans-Saharan trade was carried—'the Golden Road' which had replaced the ancient Incense and Silk Roads as the richest artery of international commerce. One can understand the excitement in the London banking circles when in September 1594 reports were received from a British agent in Marrakesh, that the gold collected for taxes in Timbuctoo amounted to sixty quintals or over three tons a year; and that in the autumn of 1599 gold worth £600,000 had arrived in Marrakesh by camel caravan from the famous Sudanese city.

Even in Shakespeare's day, then, the amount of African gold pouring into the Arab treasuries was of special interest to the commercial world, though no European trading company had been able to get control of the traffic and no white man, unless a slave, had ever been allowed to accompany the

great caravans which continually crossed and recrossed the
Sahara along the Golden Road from Timbuctoo. There was a
good reason for this prohibition—the religious hostility
between Christians and Moslems which had been engendered
by the wars of the Crusades. This hostility was so deep-
seated that fanatical Moslems refused to associate at all with
Christians, whose business affairs had to be conducted by
Jewish middlemen almost everywhere throughout Islam. The
Jew was despised, but the Christian was hated. He travelled in
Moslem countries at the risk of his life.

A second reason for the ban was the jealousy of the Arab
merchants who had a monopoly on the trans-Saharan trade.
This trade was organized as a family and tribal enterprise,
enabling the merchants of Fez, Marrakesh, Sijilmassa, and the
towns scattered throughout the whole of North Africa to
forestall outsiders from discovering the secrets of Timbuctoo,
the Niger river, and the source of the region's wealth. They
managed to do so until the beginning of the nineteenth century,
when Britain and France were determined to penetrate into the
unknown centre of Africa, and not solely for commercial
reasons either. For the end of the eighteenth and the beginning
of the nineteenth century was an age of intellectual enlighten-
ment unsurpassed in world history. And the interest in Africa
was now so profound that learned men everywhere were form-
ing societies for the express purpose of African exploration.

Notwithstanding the progress of discovery on the coasts and
borders of that vast continent [wrote Sir Joseph Banks,
President of the Royal Society in 1788], the map of the
interior is still but a wide extended blank on which the
geographer, on the authority of Leo Africanus and of the
Sherriff Edrissi the Nubian author, has traced, with a
hesitating hand, a few names of unexplored rivers and un-
certain nations.[1]

[1] *Proceedings of the African Association*, 9 June 1788, Vol I, p 6.

The African Association had to rely solely on individual travellers to elucidate the mysteries which had for so long puzzled the geographers—men like Major Alexander Gordon Laing, the first European (as far as we know) to reach Timbuctoo. Major Laing's exploration not only illustrates the spirit of the age, but the nature of travel in the Sahara as it was in 1825–6, had been for over a thousand years, and still obtains in certain areas today.

His epic journey began in Tripoli on 16 July 1825. In those days all British-sponsored trans-Saharan expeditions set out from the Libyan capital, firstly because Tripoli was the most important northern terminus of the caravan routes; and secondly because British interests were in the hands of an exceptionally able consul named Colonel Hanmer Warrington. This remarkable Englishman was appointed consul-general to what was then the Regency of Tripoli in 1814 and was quickly to become so influential that he was to all intents and purposes the actual governor of the Turkish province. In January 1825 Warrington had received instructions from Lord Bathurst of the Colonial Office to assist Major Laing of the Royal Africa Corps with his expedition to cross the Great Desert from Tripoli to Timbuctoo. Laing was thirty-two in 1825 and already a seasoned African traveller, having explored various regions of West Africa, once coming within three days' journey of the source of the Niger, which he was not allowed, however, to visit. He came, then, to Colonel Warrington and Tripoli with the full support of the Colonial Office and the African Society and was welcomed into the Warrington home as an honoured guest. It was to be a curious experience, for what began as a routine meeting between the explorer and the consul ended in the kind of story which one associates with mid-Victorian novelettes. For Colonel Warrington had a daughter, Emma, one of an unknown number of children of whom only seven, four sons and three daughters, are positively identified. Emma was evidently the second of the daughters and still in her teens when Major Laing arrived as a distinguished guest at her father's house in the suburbs of Tripoli. The handsome and distinguished soldier and the young, naive girl promptly fell in love and were actually married all within a space of six weeks. Laing and Emma, in fact, were married two days before he set out for Timbuctoo. The wedding was performed by the bride's father, and the consummation of the marriage interdicted by the same officiant. And the reason for the interdiction lies in the character of Colonel Warrington, thus described by his colleague Pellisier de Reynaud, the French consul-general in Tripoli:

> Mr. Warrington was a passionate, violent man, subject to Bacchic excitements . . . He married a natural daughter of King George IV, Jeanne-Eliza Price, and it is probable that this alliance was responsible for the post the authorities arranged on his behalf. Unlike his colleagues, he did not inhabit a villa in Tripoli itself, but built a pleasant house outside in the middle of a palmery. He meddled in local politics and with his clique was continually at war with the people of Tripoli.[1]

Here, of course, we have the gossipy account of an anglophobe Frenchman denigrating a rival who was famous through the length and breadth of North Africa; but the characterization, nonetheless, certainly sounds half-true. Perhaps instead of using such adjectives as 'passionate' and 'violent', we would today describe the British consul as a typical product of his age, which in his case spanned the Regency and Victorian eras. His own account of his exploits during the Peninsular War, for instance, is written in the characteristic style of a 'Regency buck': he writes thus to Lord Bathurst in a letter dated 24 March 1826.

[1] A letter from Pellisier de Reynaud to Augustin Bernard, dated 20 December 1850. There appears to be corroborating evidence that Warrington's wife, Jane Eliza, actually was an illegitimate daughter of the Regent.

I was sent to Spain with the rank of Lt. Col. & immediately went on that unfortunate Expedition to Fangarola and Malaga. In the Charge for the Retaking of the British guns, I was a Hundred Yards in advance of the 89th Regt and consequently the first in the French Battery where I had my Horse killed under me, and received Two Balls through my Coat . . .[1]

But the same man who writes thus, giving the impression of a devil-may-care cavalryman was, in civilian life, very much the stern *paterfamilias*, who seems to have caused great unhappiness to a family typically numerous and submissive in the mid-Victorian fashion. And it is little wonder that Emma at once fell in love with the young major who represented the outside world and offered an opportunity to live a life of her own. Colonel Warrington, in his role as consul, married his daughter, and then in his role as 'deeply religious man' (meaning that he insisted upon morning prayers and Bible readings in his study), made quite sure that the newly-wed couple were never left alone together. Consequently the marriage was never consummated, and all Laing ever really knew of his young wife was an occasional letter, the last of which he never received, for by then he had been murdered in the desert.

In contrast to Emma's loving letters, Laing seems to have had only an occasional reference to Emma from his father-in-law, who wrote, characteristically, 'Your wife, dear Emma, you may believe me is well and happy as it is her duty to be . . . It is very natural she should wish to see you & it is very probable she might resort to every argument to induce you to return, but for Heaven sake do not let your powerful feelings operate on you so as to adopt a proceeding which you would for ever repent.'[2]

---

[1] *The Letters of Major Alexander Gordon Laing 1824–26.* The Hakluyt Society. Mission to the Niger, 1944, Vol 1, p 98.
[2] *Ibid.*

Laing did not, of course, turn back. He was a soldier, and he considered it not only his duty to complete his mission, but his longed-for opportunity to obtain fame and fortune. The prize was Timbuctoo, and, just as important, a survey of the road that led thither, for both Britain and France were anxious to discover the way to the legendary city as quickly as possible. Laing, therefore, set off for Timbuctoo by way of Ghadames, a typical Saharan oasis not easy to reach even today. Ghadames is fortunate in possessing a pleasant hostelry in the centre of the town, which is virtually unchanged since Laing arrived on 13 September 1825. Thirty-five years later, the young French explorer, Henri Duveyrier, lived here with his black mistress in a house still standing. Laing, longing to be with his adored Emma, had little inclination, as the nineteen-year-old Duveyrier did, to flirt with the Tuareg girls; but he worked conscientiously to survey and describe the town, noting the remains of seven Roman tombs whose architecture, he writes, is 'extremely rude, the stones heaped upon one another in so careless a manner that I should not have considered them of Roman construction had I not discovered on digging around there several broken sarcophagi with the buried remains of the dead'. Ghadames, in fact, was the Roman *Cydamus*, a fort of that Third Augusta Legion which policed the whole of Roman North Africa for some 500 years.

From Ghadames in Libya, Laing wrote on 3 November 1825 to his father-in-law: 'please God I shall sleep in the long-looked for city [Timbuctoo] in forty-two days more.' The forty-two days were to become over 300, not far short of a year, and they were ten months of terrible tribulations.

But Laing set off with high hopes indeed, marching first south, then west, with his small caravan of six pack-camels and four *mehari*, or riding-camels, travelling along an ancient caravan route at the rather leisurely rate of twenty-odd miles a day. All went well as far as In Salah in Algeria, where the explorer wrote one of the few gay letters he was to pen: the letter is a description of his reception in the oasis where literally thousands of people had come to see this extraordinary person, asking 'Is he white?' 'Is his hair like a Turk's?' 'Has he a beard?' 'Can he fire a gun without a flint?' In fact, the women so crowded upon him that the local sheik had to rebuke them with the threat of not letting them see the Englishman again unless they stopped bothering him. 'What a sad thing it is to be a Lion,' Laing writes, perhaps hoping that his beloved Emma would be just a little jealous.

But there was one incident that took place in In Salah which was exceedingly ominous and which had a devastating effect on all future explorations in Africa.

An extremely ridiculous report has gone abroad here that I am no less a personage than Mungo Park, the Christian who made war upon the people inhabiting the banks of the Niger, who killed several, and wounded many of the Tuareg . . . Yet when I inform you that there is a Targi [singular of Tuareg] in this place who received a musket-shot in his cheek in a rencontre with Park's vessel . . . I cannot view without some apprehension the difficulties in which it may involve me.

How imprudent, how unthinking—I may even say how selfish was it in Park to attempt making discovery in this land at the expense of the blood of its inhabitants. How unjustified was such conduct! What answer am I to make to the questions which will be often put to me? What right had your countrymen to fire upon and kill our people?[1]

It would be impossible to put in fewer or more pregnant words the entire history of colonial conquest than this.

After leaving In Salah in the company of a relatively small caravan of some forty-five merchants and several hundred camels, Laing's party, which included his personal servant Jack

[1] *Laing, op cit*, p 294.

and two British sailors, travelled a steady twenty miles a day
across the Tanezrouft, one of the most arid and dreaded zones
of the Sahara. However, it was not so much the terrors of the
desert which disturbed the caravaners as the presence in the
area of the Ulad D'leim, a tribe of Tuareg based on the Hoggar
mountains to the east of the Tanezrouft. Laing dismissed this
threat as exaggerated: 'Every acacia tree in the distance being
magnified or rather metamorphosed by the apprehensive
merchants into troops of armed foes.' But the merchants were
right, for they knew the Tuareg as Laing certainly did not,
though he was soon to learn what manner of men they were.
We have an idea of the methods used by these Veiled Men from
the description of an attack on Laing given by an eyewitness,
as well as in a letter written by the explorer himself. It is a
terrible story that illustrates more vividly the dangers of desert
travel than any statistics of even great disasters involving the
loss of entire caravans.

Here is Laing's account to the consul Warrington in his
letter written from a place he calls 'Blad Sidi Mahomed' (not
yet located with certainty, but probably an encampment some
130 miles north of Timbuctoo) and dated 10 May 1826:

When I write from Timbuctoo, I shall detail precisely how
I was betrayed and nearly murdered in my sleep. In the
meantime, I shall acquaint you with the number and nature
of my wounds, in all amounting to twenty-four, eighteen of
which are exceedingly severe.

To begin from the top. I have five sabre cuts on the crown
of the head and three in the left temple, all fractures from
which much bone has come away; one on my left cheek
which fractured the jawbone and has divided the ear, form-
ing a very unsightly wound; one over the right temple and
a dreadful gash on the back of the neck, which slightly
scratched the windpipe [the spine?]; a musket ball in the
hip, which made its way through my back, slightly grazing

the backbone; five sabre cuts on my right arm and hand, three of the fingers broken, the hand cut three fourths across and the wrist bone cut through; three cuts on the left arm, the bone of which has been broken but is again uniting. One slight wound on the right leg, and two ditto with one dreadful gash on the left, to say nothing of a cut across the fingers of my left hand, now healed up . . .

As I write with my left hand with much pain and difficulty, I shall not upon that account communicate till my arrival at Timbuctoo.

Laing's camel driver, Mahommed, was an eyewitness of the Tuareg attack which began at 3 o'clock in the morning when the Major was asleep in his tent. Laing and his party had joined a southbound caravan at In Salah. Sixteen days out from this oasis, the caravaners were joined by twenty Tuareg on their racing camels, and all the Arabs, certainly, must have known that something was afoot, since the Veiled Men did not travel with slow-moving caravans for the fun of it. And so when the attack on Laing began at 3 in the morning, mounted by the twenty tribesmen armed with guns as well as their traditional swords, spears, and daggers (*les armes blanches*), the Englishmen—Laing, his servant Jack, and the two sailors, Roger and Harris—had no opportunity of adequately defending themselves. After the Tuareg had first fired into Laing's tent, they burst in and attacked him with their swords. It was during this stage of the fight that the explorer received the numerous wounds he mentions, so many, in fact, that his assailants left him for dead and went off to loot his baggage—loot, of course, being the object of their murderous attack. In the meantime, his interpreter, a Libyan Jew called Abraham Nahum, and his servant Jack managed to escape into the darkness. The sailor Roger, who seems to have fought back, though like Laing he was unarmed, was hacked to death. The other sailor, Harris, was shot in the leg, but crawled away to the tent of the captain of the caravan, the sheik Babani. The Jewish interpreter Nahum was now caught and dispatched by the swords of the Tuareg, who then proceeded to rob the explorer of almost everything he possessed, notably all the funds kept in his strong box to pay the considerable expenses of the expedition. Thus, two of the party were killed, Major Laing was near to death from his wounds, Harris had a leg broken by a bullet, and only Jack had escaped unscathed.

Later the caravan master, sheik Babani, was accused of collusion with the Tuaregs in this dastardly incident, cowardly even for the Veiled Men, who were later to murder Alexandrine Tinne, the Danish woman explorer, in similar circumstances; but since Babani did manage to lead Laing and those of his party who survived to the safety of the sheik Muktar's encampment farther south on the road to Timbuctoo, the accusations of perfidy seem unjustified. In any case, it was an astonishing achievement, both for Babani as master of the caravan and for the desperately wounded Laing, who had to be tied to the back of a camel, to have continued a journey requiring unimaginable fortitude.

Laing partially recovered from his wounds at sheik Muktar's encampment—at least he stemmed his bleeding, patched up his cuts, and waited for his broken bones to knit. His right arm and hand, however, were now useless. But even so, he was determined to finish his mission and to reach Timbuctoo. But now Muktar's village was struck by typhoid and within a few days, the sheik Babani, Jack the servant, and Harris the sailor were all dead. Laing was finally alone in the desert, though within a hundred miles of his goal.

Any man with less resolution—one might truthfully say, less obsessed—would have turned back even now, since everybody in the area, including Laing's friends, knew that the new dictator of Timbuctoo, Sultan Mohammed Bello, was fanatically hostile to Europeans in general and Christians in particular, on the grounds that such men would be 'mischievous and the cause of perpetual war.' However, sheik Muktar, an Arab of the most honourable type found in the true desert, undertook to send the Englishman to whom he had given sanctuary to Timbuctoo with an armed escort, and to recommend him to the consideration of his friends. As a result, Laing finally entered the legendary city on 13 August 1826, was hospitably received, and even advanced enough money to continue his journey when the time came to leave.

On a house in Timbuctoo a plaque records the residence of Major Alexander Gordon Laing from 13 August to 22 September 1826. What did he accomplish in those forty days that he stayed here? All that remains is one letter written from Timbuctoo, for all his precious journals and maps were burnt or thrown away at the time of his murder. His letter, dated 21 September 1826, tells us very little, except that his life was again in danger. He writes 'my perils are not yet at an end,' meaning, as we know now, that he had had the bad luck to arrive in Timbuctoo when religious fanatics were inflaming the perpetual tribal quarrels of the region. Laing as both a Christian and a European was in double jeopardy, since orders for his expulsion had come from Sultan Bello, chief of the Fulani who, in general, controlled the area. Sultan Bello suspected the English of wanting to conquer the Sudan as, he said, they had conquered India, so there was a political motive for expelling Laing. Politics and religion are, of course, inextricably intertwined in Moslem countries, and this suspicion of the Englishman became outright hatred of an infidel.

However, during the forty days that Laing lived in Timbuctoo, he managed to get a very fair idea of the layout of the city, visited Kabara, the port of Timbuctoo on the Niger, and hence saw that the river flowed eastwards. More important, he had, according to his own report, 'been busily employed searching the records of the town, which are abundant . . . Nor is it with any common degree of satisfaction that I say my perseverance has been amply rewarded.'

9

So it would seem that Laing actually learnt a great deal of the history of the mysterious Sudanese capital and was hence in a position to describe to an eager world the truth or falsity of the myth of the 'golden city' which lay at the end of the Caravan Road. How he was murdered is revealed in the testimony of a black slave whom he had liberated, a man called Bungola. The evidence will be found in the Laing Papers of the Royal Society. Here is the pertinent part:

Bungola: On the third day, at night, the Arabs of the country attacked and killed my master.

The British Consul (*Warrington*): Was the attack on the Koffle [caravan] or only against your master?

B: I do not know.

W: Was anyone killed beside your master?

B: I was wounded, but cannot say if any were killed.

W: Were you sleeping alongside your master?

B: Yes.

W: How many wounds had your master?

B: Cannot say, but all with swords. And in the morning saw his head cut off.

W: What property had your master when he was killed?

B: Two camels. One carried the provisions. The other carried my master and his bags.

The murder took place under a tree, where almost a hundred years later the skeletons of a white man and an Arab boy were found by a French investigating expedition.[1] There seems no reason to doubt that the bones were those of Major Alexander Gordon Laing, whose remains were taken back to Timbuctoo and buried in the European cemetery there.

Emma's last letter, written after hearing about the Tuareg attack in the desert, never reached Laing. It is a passionate and beautiful letter which tells us a great deal about Emma, and it is a moving epitaph to their brief and tragic marriage:

[1] A. Bonnel de Mezières, *Le Major A. Gordon Laing*. Larose, Paris, 1927.

Tripoli 10th Nov. 1826

Oh my beloved dearest Laing, alas alas what have you been exposed to, what suffering, to have saved you one pang I would with joy have shed every drop of blood that warms this heart—Had I been with you in that fearful moment my arms which would have encircled you might for some time have shielded you from the swords of those Daemons [i.e. the Tuareg]—My beloved Laing sorrow has laid a heavy hand on your Emma's head & so it has on yours—Alas Laing how cruel how sad has been our fate—Are we destined to endure more misery, or will a kind providence at length pity our unhappiness and restore us to each other— Will you my own idolised husband return to your Emma's fond arms, will you come & repose on her faithful bosom—

Never for a moment my beloved Laing have you been absent from my thoughts. You have been present to my imagination waking & sleeping—You will find your Emma the same in heart and soul as when you last embraced her, entirely and for ever devoted to her Laing.

Adieu my best beloved, may heaven soon restore you to the arms of your ever adoring wife,

Emma M Gordon Laing[1]

Laing's journey marked the end of the mystery of Timbuctoo, which was again reached two years later, in 1828, by the French traveller, René Caillié. And what did he find when he got there?

I had formed a totally different view of the grandeur and wealth of Timbuctoo. The city presented, at first view, nothing but a mass of ill-looking houses built of earth.[2]

In fact, Timbuctoo is now, and always has been, a drab and ill-built town, looking as though it had been thrown down in

---

[1] *Laing, op cit.*
[2] Caillié, *op cit*, p 41.

the middle of the desert. So it looked to the first Arab travellers who visited it, and so it looks today. Its charm to the modern tourist, who can now arrive by commercial aeroplane if he so wishes, is the very plainness of a city universally renowned, yet not even possessing a bank, or a second-class hostelry, let alone a theatre, cinema, or place of entertainment. The streets are still thoroughfares in the sand, as they have always been; the houses are still constructed of mud-bricks; the water is still drawn from wells; the caravans still arrive and camp on the outskirts; the place is still almost completely without goods and resources, except those that arrive from outside.

Of the great caravan roads which radiated out from the city, crossing the Sahara on north-south routes and following the Niger river on the east-west axis, several survive to this day, and even though the main Tanezrouft and Hoggar trails are now travelled by motor vehicles, the road Major Laing marched down is still the way of the camel caravans, though these *azalai* are seen less and less as the big German diesel-powered lorries take over the conveyance of trading goods.

Timbuctoo itself is no longer the southern terminus of the Golden Road. The visitor must not expect, therefore, to see 'the rich King of Timbukto who hath many plates and sceptres of gold and who keeps a magnificent and well-furnished court', as Leo Africanus wrote in the middle of the sixteenth century. Kings like Mansa Musa, the Mandingo emperor of Mali, and Askai the Great, ruler of the Songhai, and even Bello, the Sultan of the Fulani, are as remote from the modern world as the medieval emperors of Europe.

Even so, such is the romance that attaches to the very name Timbuctoo that the traveller, provided he is not accompanied by a train of sightseers weighed down with cameras, can still feel the aura of the most famous place in Africa—a city along whose streets walked the greatest Saharan explorers of the nineteenth century.

10

The Pilgrim Caravans

One of the oldest functions of the caravan trade was the transport of pilgrims to religious shrines, many of which, like the oracle of Zeus Ammon in the Siwa oasis of the Western Desert, could only be reached by a camel train. At the same time, most of the sacred sites of the pagan world were busy, populous places situated on the international caravan routes, and here religion, commerce, and pleasure combined in and around the temples. Herodotus observed this on his visit to Babylon, where the worship of the god Marduk was concomitant with prostitution conducted within the precincts of the *ziggurat*; and inasmuch as every Babylonian woman, according to the Greek historian, had to do a spell in this peculiar line of religious duty, one may assume that Marduk was a very popular deity and that the old city was always thronged with eager pilgrims. Indeed, similar temples, sanctuaries, and shrines abounded all over the pagan world, the more renowned, naturally, being dedicated to fertility goddesses like Atargatis at Hieropolis in Syria; Astarte at Sidon and Tyre; Aphrodite and Venus in every larger Greek and Roman city. Pilgrims thronged to these centres for uplift, and in many cases had to join a caravan in order to reach them.

The caravan, therefore, has played a key role in the history of religion, since it enabled the adherents of the many diverse cults to disseminate their beliefs either actively as missionaries, or passively, as travellers. Initially Christianity seems to have spread throughout the Mediterranean world as a result of the activities of the latter class: it was Jewish commercial travellers who brought word of a Messiah named Jesus Christ to the

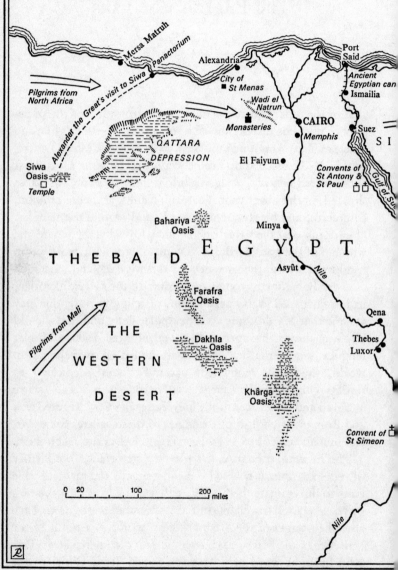

Pilgrim Caravans

MEDITERRANEAN SEA

Mersa Matruh

Panactorium

Alexandria

Port Said

City of St Menas

Ancient Egyptian can

Ismailia

→ Pilgrims from North Africa

Wadi el Natrun

Monasteries

CAIRO

Suez

S I

Alexander the Great's visit to Siwa

QATTARA DEPRESSION

Memphis

El Faiyum

Convents of St Antony & St Paul

Gulf of Su

Siwa Oasis

Temple

Bahariya Oasis

Minya

E G Y P T

T H E B A I D

Farafra Oasis

Asyût

Nile

Qena

→ Pilgrims from Mali

T H E

Dakhla Oasis

Thebes

Luxor

W E S T E R N

Khârga Oasis

D E S E R T

Convent of St Simeon

0 20   100   200 miles

Nile

Roman-hating natives of the Mediterranean ports. Along the Asian caravan trails evangelists brought old or new creeds to peoples the West had scarcely even heard of, so that in lands as remote as China were found converts to Judaism, Christianity, Islam, and Buddhism.

The dissemination of Buddhism is a classic example of spread of ideas along caravan trails, for historians now generally agree that the Indian religion reached the Central Asian kingdoms of Sogdiana, Bactriana, and Khotan, as well as Tibet and China, along the Silk Road. Christian missionaries also used this international highway to spread their gospel throughout the whole of Asia, as in the West they brought it to the pagans of northern Europe by following the merchants along the ancient roads which had always linked the Baltic with the Mediterranean. And, in due course, the long-distance caravans came to include pilgrims visiting the shrines of their particular gods—Chinese Buddhists travelling to the sacred sites in Tibet, India, and Afghanistan; Christian priests and nuns setting out from monasteries in Europe for the Holy Land; Asians and Africans converging on Mecca and Medina—all of them, until the beginning of our own era, relying for their transport and safe conduct on the caravan.

The constant coming and going of pilgrim caravans along the highways of the pagan world had tended to die out with the inception of Christianity, since the first converts to that religion had neither temples, sanctuaries, nor sacred shrines to visit. God was worshipped in spirit and in truth wherever two or three were gathered together. Far from going in companies on pilgrimages, the zealous betook themselves to lonely places in the mountains and deserts and, in some cases, unable to find a hole in the ground in which to hide, appropriated a high pillar upon which to perch out of reach of their fellows. But such piety created in itself the longing in other devout Christians to go and see holy men who had been living in a cave for forty years or standing on the plinth of a column with-

out ever lying down at all. And eventually the sites where the
ascetics had mortified themselves, where the Jewish patriarchs
had laid down the law, and where the apostles, saints, and
martyrs had been scourged, crucified, or boiled alive, all became
the goals of pilgrims. Indeed, the pilgrimage industry soon became so extensive that prepaid and guided tours were organized,
especially in those parts of Africa and the Middle East where
travel has always been hazardous. The caravan trade in the
deserts of Sinai and Egypt profited greatly from the longing of
pious folk to visit the cells of famous hermits like Macarius,
Serapion, Paul, and Antony. Among the first of these pilgrims
was the Lady Paula, a Roman matron of ancient lineage, great
wealth, and a high social rank, a disciple together with her
daughter Eustochium, of Jerome. These three set off on a
pilgrimage to Jerusalem and the Thebaid in the spring of
AD 382, and from Gaza in Palestine took the old Incense Road
to Alexandria. From Alexandria they crossed the desert to
Nitria, today the Wadi el Natrun, in company with other
pilgrims and sightseers.

> Whose cell did she [Paula, the Roman matron] not enter?
> At whose feet did she not prostrate herself? Through each
> of the holy men she believed herself to see Christ. Her zeal
> was wonderful—her courage scarcely credible for a woman.
> Forgetful of her sex and the weakness of her frame, she
> desired to dwell with her maidens among so many thousands
> of monks. And perhaps, as all invited her, she would have
> obtained her desire, had not a greater longing for the holy
> places drawn her back.[1]

The Roman lady Paula was followed a few years later by the
French nun, Saint Silvia of Aquitaine, who has left us an
account of her travels in a long letter home to her conventual

[1] St Jerome, *The Pilgrimage of the Holy Paula*, translated by Aubrey Stewart.
Palestine Pilgrims Text Society. London, 1887, Vol 1, p 16.

sisters. Silvia enjoyed her tour of the Holy Land immensely, so much so that scholars have asked 'Who is Silvia? What is she?' since the only Silvia of the period we can positively identify was a women ascetic who, according to Palladius, the historian of the Egyptian hermits, decribed herself as follows:

> I am now sixty years of age; but except for the tips of my fingers (and that for the purpose of communicating) no water has ever touched my face, or my feet, or any of my limbs. Even when, being seized with various diseases, I was urged by the physicians to take a bath, I could not endure to give flesh its due. I have never slept on a couch or travelled in a litter.[1]

But the authoress of *The Pilgrimage* states rather petulantly that she had to walk up the slopes of Mount Sinai instead of being carried up in a chair; and, she adds, 'You do not go up gradually by a spiral path, but you go straight up as if up the face of a wall.' This does not sound like Saint Silvia the ascetic, but the complaint of a well-to-do tourist prepared to pay a *supplément* for a few extra comforts. So no doubt the French nun rode in a *shibriyah*, or wicker cage, still used for transporting women in Moslem countries, though considering the way these top-heavy litters slip and slide about, sometimes turning a complete somersault with the passenger inside, the nun might have preferred to walk beside her camel from Mount Sinai along the shores of the Red Sea to Suez.

From the fourth century AD, then, the pilgrim industry throughout the eastern Mediterranean gave a considerable boost to the caravan trade which by this time had lost much of its international traffic, due to the increase of maritime freightage between the East and the West. Once the Roman legions had enforced the *pax romana* on land, the sea, too,

---

[1] Palladius, *The Lausiac History*. Newman Press: Westminster, Md. Ancient Christian Writers. No 34, p 196.

became safer for merchant ships which now brought the products of the Orient, including Chinese silk, across the oceans to harbours on the Egyptian side of the Gulf of Suez. As a result, the great spice caravans of Arabia now lost a considerable tonnage of cargo, and the camels were moved north to cater for the growing pilgrim trade.

How great that trade was 1,500 years ago is illustrated dramatically by the existence of the once lost City of St Menas, the great Christian shrine fifty miles south-west of Alexandria, which actually disappeared for a thousand years.[1] For after about AD 1000, nobody even knew the site of the City of St Menas, and some doubted whether the place had ever existed at all, despite the fact that most of the national museums of Europe possessed those little earthenware flasks, or ampullas, with a crude portrait of St Menas standing between two camels and the inscription *Blessing of St Menas*, souvenirs brought back by pilgrims from the bazaars of the city. In 1905 the site was finally located by the German archaeologist Monsignor Carl-Maria Kaufmann, who excavated the great cathedral of Arcadius and the surrounding buildings, revealing a sizeable city of basilicas, baths, rest houses, and public buildings dedicated to the needs of thousands of pilgrims who crossed the desert to worship at the shrine of Menas, purchased a flask full of holy water, and so returned to their homelands.

Arduous though conditions must have been for the Europeans who travelled with the caravans to desert shrines like the City of St Menas and the Nitrian monasteries, their pilgrimages were in the nature of a holiday tour compared with the *hadj* enjoined upon all adult Moslems, irrespective of nationality or sex. To travel from London to Jerusalem in the time of the emperor Septimius Severus was as easy, safe, and agreeable as a trip between English counties today. But to

[1] See 'The Lost City' in James Wellard's *Desert Pilgrimage*. London: Hutchinson, 1970, Chapter 11, pp 136–147.

travel to Mecca from anywhere was always, until the inception of international airways, a long, arduous, and dangerous venture. So difficult, in fact, was the journey undertaken by the pilgrims of the great Syrian, Iraqi, and Egyptian caravans, that it is estimated one-third of the travellers and animals died on the passage. Nonetheless, the prophet had decreed that a visit to the Ka'aba was a sacred duty to Allah, even though the Ka'aba itself was originally a characteristic heathen sanctuary within which the local gods had been housed in the form of idols. Mohammed, after he had accepted the Jahweh and the prophets of the Jews, declared the ancient shrine to be the work of Abraham and Ishmael and not of the heathens and decreed that the faithful should pray towards Mecca instead of Jerusalem. The pagan idols and pictures were ejected from the building, which was now left empty save for the gold and silver lamps which still illuminate the Black Stone, the holiest relic of Islam, corresponding, one could say, to the cross of the Christians. It was the Black Stone which was given to Adam on his expulsion from paradise in order to obtain forgiveness of his sins: hence he who touches and kisses the Stone has fulfilled his 'duty to Allah', has faithfully performed his *hadj*, and has the promise of salvation in the after-life.

Once Islamic law had decreed that all adult Moslems had an obligation to make their pilgrimage to the holy shrine of Mecca at least once in their lifetime, the international caravan routes were to be busy for thirteen centuries with a traffic involving the migration of hundreds of thousands of people from every direction, all converging on a small town in central Arabia, some coming by boat, some on horses or mules, some in litters, but the great majority with camel caravans. Of these the three principal formations were the Syrian Caravan, which set out from Constantinople and proceeded via Damascus to Mecca; the Egyptian Caravan, which started from Cairo, crossed Sinai to Aqaba, and marched southwards to Mecca down the old Incense Road; and the Iraqi Caravan which cut across Arabia via one of the lateral routes of the same Incense Road.

There are a number of descriptions by Europeans of what life was like for the Mecca pilgrim, for although an infidel caught in the vicinity of the Ka'aba could well get himself stoned to death as a spy and blasphemer, Christians in disguise had been making the famous *hadj* certainly from as early as 1503, when Lodovico Barthema of Bologna reached the holy city from Damascus, travelling with the Syrian Caravan. In 1678, Joseph Pitts, an English seaman enslaved by the Algerians and forced under torture to repeat the formula of submission to Mohammed, accompanied his master on the pilgrimage to Mecca via the Egyptian Caravan, an experience which he described on his return to his home in Exeter. John Lewis Burckhardt reached Mecca in 1814; Richard Burton in 1853; and T. F. Keane in 1877.

The last of these describes how he was nearly unmasked as a Christian when 'some great hulking brute' approached him, saying, 'Christian dog, if you are Mohammedan make the profession of your faith,' whereupon the Englishman took hold of this stranger by the shoulders, swung him round, and kicked him hard on the backside. Result: the bystanders started stoning Keane, one of them a tiny Arab boy who, while struggling to heave a rock he could scarcely lift, was picked up by the Englishman, carried to a wall, and used as a shield against the stone-throwers. But even though the Englishman escaped, he felt it safer to go into hiding for three weeks, as once the rumour got about that there was a Christian in disguise in the holy city, he was in constant danger. Keane tells us that he passed the time smoking opium and that three weeks passed like three days, while the chanting of the pilgrims that went on continously night and day under his window, began to sound like some charming English madrigals. 'In short,' he adds, 'I did not know a moment's discomfort the whole time.'[1]

[1] T. F. Keane, *Six Months in Meccah*, London: Tinsley Brothers, 1881, pp 60-5.

From what Keane heard while he was in Mecca, there were evidently other disguised Christians who had arrived with the pilgrim caravans, only to have been captured, though what their fate was he never knew. A great deal—in fact, everything—depended on how well-versed the Christian imposter was in the prayers and rituals of Islam, as well as the Arabic language, for there was a period when it was a crime to speak any other tongue than that of the Prophet in Mecca or Medina.

The first European to record a pilgrimage to Mecca was the Italian traveller Lodovico Barthema. This extraordinary man (assuming he is not another Baron Munchausen) states that he deliberately became a Mameluke, or renegade Christian, in Damascus in order to join the great Caravan that was leaving for Mecca on 8 April 1503. This *azalai* that year consisted of 40–50,000 pilgrims, 35,000 camels, and thousands of horses and asses. It was escorted by a troop of sixty Mamelukes, of whom Barthema was now one. Sixty men seems few enough to protect 40,000 pilgrims, particularly as the caravan was frequently ambushed by Bedouin on arrival at the wells. But, says the Italian:

> We always had to fight with a vast number of Arabs [Bedouin], but they never killed more than one man and one lady, for we sixty Mamelukes were sufficient defence against forty or fifty thousand Arabs.[1]

Barthema tells us that the journey from Damascus to Mecca took forty days. The day's march often consisted of twenty hours of almost continuous travel, followed by twenty-four hours' rest. The camels were then fed 'five loaves of barley meal, uncooked, and each of about the size of a pomegranate', a curious diet for camels, who were watered every three days at wells often dug out by the caravaners. Sometimes, as has

[1] *The Itinerary of Lodovico di Barthema of Bologna from 1502 to 1508*, translated from the original Italian by John Winter Jones. The Argonaut Press: London, 1928, p 13.

happened with caravans from the beginning of time, the wells were dry. Then men and animals collapsed in considerable numbers, the former, according to Barthema, being left to die from thirst as the caravan moved on to the next water-hole. But every time this vast concourse reached a well, the local tribesmen attempted to drive them off, for the obvious reason that such numbers of thirsty men and beasts would drain the wells dry. This, according to Barthema, was where the sixty Mamelukes went into action, at one well fighting off 24,000 Arabs and killing 1,600 of them; and at another confronting '5000 Jews who go naked, live entirely upon the flesh of sheep, are circumcised, and if they can get a Moor [i.e. an Arab] into their hands, they skin him alive.' It was in this region that 'some of the men drank so much water that they burst,'—another tall story, though every desert traveller knows from experience that anyone who tries to quench his thirst by continually drinking will end up feeling as if this is precisely what is going to happen to him.

Barthema gives us a good picture of the great Damascus Caravan at the beginning of the sixteenth century. The Englishman Joseph Pitts does the same for the Cairo Caravan at the end of the seventeenth. Pitts was a converted slave, forced through cruelties to pronounce the required formula. Once he had pronounced it, he was accepted as a believer by his new master, a kind old man who took him from Algiers to Cairo where they joined the Mecca-bound pilgrims.

The Cairo Caravan, Pitts says, was 'joined by great multitudes'; in other words, by all the pilgrim caravans arriving from every part of Moslem Africa, one section coming from Morocco and the far west; another from the western Sudan; and a third from Nubia and the south. When all these tributaries had merged into the main stream, the pilgrims set out, taking with them the curtain of black brocade traditionally woven in the Egyptian capital and annually brought to Mecca to replace the old covering on the Ka'aba. Pitts tells us that the pilgrims were beset by dangers from the moment they set out. Their boat sailing up the Nile from Alexandria to Cairo was attacked by river pirates, and in Cairo itself the travellers were waylaid by:

'courtesans who wear their hair in tresses behind, reaching down to their very heels, with little bells at the end, which swing against their heels, and make a tinkling sound as they go . . . These madams go along the streets, smoking their pipes of from four to five feet long; and when they sit at their doors, a man can scarce pass by but they will endeavour to decoy him in . . . I am told that for three or four pence any man may gratify his lust upon them. But they are so cunning that they will not allow any to stay longer with them in the act and payment for it; because they will be ready for a fresh gallant.'[1]

One must say that Pitts's madams 'smoking pipes five feet long' represent one of the more curious hazards of the *hadj*, though far less dangerous than the sturdy rogues who 'fall on a stranger at midday and rob him and beat him to that degree that it hath cost him his life.'

We learn from Pitts how a great religious caravan marched. It was divided into companies, each with its own name and company commander and attendant camels. The camels were tied four abreast, rank upon rank, thousands of them thus marching like a well-disciplined army. At their head went the officer commanding carried in a litter slung between two camels, one in front, one behind. If this man had his wife or wives with him, they travelled in the same manner. Following the company commander came his sumpter camel, a huge beast which carried his treasure, clothing, supplies, and so forth. On each side of this camel hung two large bells 'which may be heard a long way off'. Many of the other camels had smaller

[1] *The Red Sea . . . as described by Joseph Pitts*, ed. by Sir William Foster, CIE. London: Printed for the Hakluyt Society, 1949, p 12.

bells attached to their necks and legs; and, says Pitts, 'the tinkling of all these bells and the singing of the camel-drivers make the journey pass away delightfully.'

Most of the travelling was, of course, done at night when the caravan moved slowly across the desert lit by hundreds of great lanterns carried on poles at the head of each company. What with the bells and the chanting in the night and the moving lights and the sibilant shuffle of tens of thousands of men and camels, the old Damascus and Cairo Caravans must be accounted among the great sights of the world—a spectacle never, of course, to be seen again. The members of this Mecca pilgrimage were continually in a state of exaltation in the satisfaction of performing their duty to God, so that even those poor pilgrims who marched without money, food, or water had no fear that Allah would not preserve them. Such paupers seldom went hungry, in fact, since the wealthier *hadjis* invariably invited them to share their meals. Pitts's master, who had stocked up enough food in Cairo to see them to Mecca and back, always included one of these mendicants in his ménage, notably an Irish renegade whose characteristic blarney had earnt him the reputation of being 'a very pious man and a great zealot.' For instance, the Irishman declared to his fellow-pilgrims that his visit to Mecca 'had brought him into a heaven upon earth'. It was no wonder he was well fed by the native Moslems.

The principal hazard of desert travel under these conditions was, of course, the possibility of a shortage of water, so that it was imperative that a good well was reached at least every third day. Another danger was 'skulking, thievish Arabs'— that is, Bedouin who preyed on the stragglers by day and the sleeping pilgrims at night. These bandits were adept at stealing a whole file of camels, for when these animals are linked nose to tail, they will follow the lead camel. At night the Bedouin crept into the outskirts of the encampment and stole what they could, including clothes. Richard Burton tells us that the young tribesmen of the Hedjaz steal not for the value of the loot, but for 'honour'.

So the pilgrims, while they were supposed to be under the protection of Allah and the Prophet, were actually subject to all the risks as well as the discomforts of the road. They could expect to be swindled by hucksters and robbed by rogues. Joseph Pitts's patron, for instance, had his silk handkerchief 'stole out of his bosom' while he was praying at the tomb of Mahommed. (One is reminded of the Christmas Eve service in Bethlehem where the pick-pockets are busy to this day, though working more in the region of the worshipper's posterior, where he keeps his wallet, than his bosom, where some still keep a handkerchief.) J. F. Keane, the Victorian traveller, noted that the holy places in and around Mecca were much frequented by sturdy beggars, the sturdiest occupying the best positions, of course; and before he left, he was not only mulcted of 'a fabulous amount of coin' by the beggars and touts, but beguiled out of his last half-piastre 'by a young Arab damsel with lovely eyes' who accompanied him into a dark passage for an encounter he does not specify.

It is Richard Burton, however, who gives the most classic of all descriptions of Mecca and the Mecca caravan as it approaches the holy city. Burton, in 1853, a lieutenant of the 18th Regiment, Bombay Native Infantry, thirty-two years of age, disguised himself as an Afghan Dervish called Shaykh Abdullah on the grounds that Dervishes include in their sect people of all nationalities, ranks, ages, and creeds. Moreover, the Dervish is allowed considerable freedom in matters of custom and ritual, even to the extent of omitting to pray at the prescribed times; and, most convenient from Burton's point of view, 'the more haughty and offensive he is to the people the more they respect him; a decided advantage to the traveller of choleric temperament.'[1]

---

[1] Sir Richard Burton, *A Pilgrimage to Al-Madinah and Meccah*, London: Herbert Joseph, 1937, p 16.

This bogus Afghan Dervish, took the route to Mecca from Cairo via the Eastern Desert to Suez, where he boarded a pilgrim ship to Arabia. The boat was built to carry a maximum of sixty passengers. Ninety-seven with all their luggage had bought—or fought—their way on board. It eventually arrived at the Arabian port of Yambu, the 'gate of the Holy City', an appellation it shared in Burton's day with Jiddah, the port nearest to Mecca. From here a party of pilgrims, Burton included, set out with a grain caravan for Medina. The explorer, who had hurt his foot, decided to ride in a *shugduf*, or litter, which was only normally used by women, children, and what he calls 'Exquisites'. It consisted of a sort of wicker cage into which Burton was supposed to climb by way of the camel's neck, the *shugduf* being placed on the back of a very tall animal. The 'Dervish', in keeping with his bad foot and choleric temper, refused to mount in this fashion and insisted that the camel kneel. (The Bedouin, incidentally, despise people who cannot mount a camel by swinging up via the neck—no easy feat.)

At Medina, Burton met up with the Damascus Caravan, which had just arrived. It was supposed to set out for Mecca on 1 September, to be followed two days later by the 'Flying Caravan' which consisted of the vigorous pilgrims mounted on trotting camels and carrying only three saddle-bags and weapons. Burton, as one would expect, had opted for the Flying Caravan; but suddenly messengers came rushing from the bazaar (centre of all news and gossip) with news that Saad the Robber refused to give a safe conduct to the pilgrims and intended 'to cut the throat of every hen that ventured into his territory'. The problem now was to recruit reliable camel-men upon a road where robberies, stabbings, demands for new and excessive tribute, and outright desertions were the rule rather than the exception. Burton was fortunate in engaging an old Bedu sheik, scarred, as usual, with wounds, but obviously a man of integrity. They set out along the road which was littered with the carcases of asses, ponies, and camels from which strips of flesh were being torn by the vultures. Great hunks of meat were also being hacked from those animals which had had their throats cut according to the Moslem ritual, the butchering being performed by those pilgrims, penniless and almost naked, who were glad of the meat whatever its condition; and so, with steaks slung over their shoulders, went stumbling along after the caravan.

At 3 o'clock each morning, the departure gun was fired and the vast concourse of men and animals began another day's journey, 7,000 pilgrims and as many beasts of burden, according to Burton. The caravan had to penetrate a narrow pass before reaching a broad plain, and here the different companies of Turks, Syrians, Persians, Arabs, and Indians jostled and pushed to get through first, so that camels were rolled over, women and children were knocked off their perches, litters smashed, while everybody yelled and shouted abuse at everybody else: in short, the customary confusion which has always characterized the first stages of the day's march. But despite much superficial chaos, the great pilgrim caravans were organized on a basis of military discipline, the times of departure and arrival, the halts along the road, and the order of marching all being directed from the pasha's, or commanding general's, headquarters by means of a cannon, whose booms were the equivalent of the military trumpet-calls.

But even though the Mecca caravans were ordered in this fashion and protected by a troop of regular soldiers, they were continually exposed to ambushes by the tribes who controlled the mountain passes and the wells. Yet the *hadj* and those participating in it were supposed to be sacrosanct, immune from all violence. The fact was that the tribes who attacked the caravans, though Moslems themselves, still insisted on their ancient territorial rights: in other words, the traveller, whether he was a pious Moslem on his pilgrimage to Mecca, or a Christian tourist visiting the ruins of Petra, had to pay customs duties to cross the tribal grazing land or to draw water from its wells. Any traveller refusing to pay the prescribed dues was liable to be killed on the spot if he resisted. So despite the admonitions of the Prophet and the threats of the sultans, the local tribes controlling the trails to Mecca held up the pilgrim caravans with impunity. The Damascus Caravan in 1853 was no exception. It was attacked by the Utaybah tribe one evening on a mountain road, two days out from Mecca. Here is Burton's description of the incident:

> Terrible confusion: women screamed, children cried, and men vociferated, each one striving with might and main to urge his animal out of the place of death. But the road being narrow, they only managed to jam the vehicles in a solid immovable mass. . . . The irregular horsemen, perfectly useless, galloped up and down over the stones, shouting to and ordering one another. The Pasha of the army had his carpet spread at the foot of the left-hand precipice and debated over his pipe with the officers what ought to be done. Then it was the conduct of the Mahhabis found favour in my eyes. They came up, galloping their camels, their elf-locks tossing in the wind, and their flaring torches casting a strange lurid light over their features. Taking up a position, one body began to fire on the Utaybah robbers, whilst two or three hundred dismounting swarmed up the hill under the guidance of Sherif Zayd. Presently the firing was heard far in our rear, the robbers having fled. The head of the column advanced, and the dense body of pilgrims opened out. Our forced halt was now exchanged for a flight . . . I had no means of ascertaining the number of men killed and wounded.[1]

To travellers today, including pilgrims whose sole risk is a bout of diarrhoea and whose chief discomfort is the lack of

[1] *Op cit*, pp 279–80.

ice-cubes for the evening *apéritif*, it is difficult to understand
the mentality of those Mecca-bound pilgrims of a hundred
years ago—of men travelling thousands of miles from as far
east as Malaysia and as far west as Senegal merely to walk
seven times round the simple stone and marble building called
the Ka'aba and to kiss the Black Stone housed within it. But
the failure to understand, let alone sympathize with, Islam is
partially due to the distrust of anything mystical; for to the
old pilgrims, Christians *en route* to Egypt and Palestine, and
Moslems *en route* to Mecca and Medina, the experience of the
journey was just as meaningful as the view of the shrine itself.
The journey meant companionship, excitement, and continual
amusement as well as spiritual uplift, particularly for the poor
and lonely; and best of all, it meant the discovery of that real
sense of brotherhood which is so characteristic of caravan
travel.

So we should not think of the pilgrims as solemn-faced and
pious travellers marching along singing hymns, their minds so
full of holy thoughts that they were not aware of their aching
feet. On the contrary, every traveller emphasizes the physical
strain of the journey under the conditions which obtained in
earlier centuries. But the reward was an adventure which
millions of insignificant individuals scattered all over the world
could not only dream of but actually experience, thanks to the
duty imposed upon them by their Prophet.

It was the English renegade, Joseph Pitts, who describes for
us what it was actually like to complete such a pilgrimage and
to behold the holy shrine, the bourne of so many incredible
journeys:

At the very first sight of the House of God [writes Pitts],
the pilgrims melt into tears. . . . And I profess I could not
choose but admire to see those poor creatures so extraordinarily devout and affectionate when they were about
these superstitions [performing the rituals of worship], and

with what awe, insomuch that I could scare forbear shedding of tears to see their zeal, though blind and idolatrous.[1]

To this Richard Burton adds that he, too, had a moment of profound emotion when at 1 o'clock in the morning a great cry arose from the vanguard of the caravan, 'Mecca! Mecca! The Sanctuary! O the Sanctuary!' and he looked out from his litter and saw by the light of the desert stars the dim outline of the holy city.

[1] Pitts, *op cit*, p 23.

11

Military Caravans
The Camel in Desert Warfare

Nasir screamed at me, 'Come on', with his bloody mouth; and we plunged our camels madly over the hill, and down towards the head of the fleeing enemy. The slope was too steep for a camel-gallop, but steep enough to make their pace terrific and the course uncontrollable ... My camel, the Sherari racer, Naama, stretched herself out and hurled downhill with such might that we soon outdistanced the others. The Turks fired a few shots, but mostly only shrieked and turned to run: the bullets they did send us were not very harmful, for it took much to bring a charging camel down in a dead heap.[1]

Thus Lawrence of Arabia describes a camel charge at the end of his historic march in the summer of 1917 across the desert of Sha'fat in Jad, when the Turkish fort Aqaba was taken from the rear. With heroics like this, it is no wonder that camel-riders took on a new status in popular military history.

Yet Lawrence was not describing anything new in the art of war, for that Arab raid across the desert happens to coincide with the earliest accounts of battles that we have. The annals of the Sumerians speak of camel-riding nomads who came out of the Arabian Desert and overthrew the city of Ur in 2100 BC. These tribesmen were the first to capture and tame the wild camel, which they used not to carry loads, but to wage war in precisely the same fashion that Lawrence describes in the famous charge on Aqaba.

[1] T. E. Lawrence, *Seven Pillars of Wisdom*, Penguin Modern Classics 1962, p 310.

Camel-riders, in fact, had begun to determine the rise and fall of the Middle Eastern empires from the third millennium BC, and are frequently referred to in the oldest cuneiform sources. The Old Testament, too, records that a nomadic people called the Midianites conquered Israel and the whole of Palestine: 'They came as grasshoppers, for both they and their camels were without number.'[1]

The lesson taught by these obscure desert tribesmen was not lost on the nations of Mesopotamia who rose to imperial power. From the mid-eighth century BC, the Assyrians, who had relied on two-wheeled, horse-drawn chariots for their wars in the mountains of Armenia, turned to camels for their drive south to the Persian Gulf; and by the sixth century the Persians under Cyrus had learnt that chariots, and even cavalry, were vulnerable against disciplined infantrymen, massed in ranks ten to thirty lines deep, and armed with pikes eight to ten feet long; and that heavy masses of men and weapons were in-effective in desert terrain—as his successor, Cambyses, dis-covered on losing an army of 50,000 men in the Western Desert of Egypt.

The Romans, at first unfamiliar with desert warfare, were surprisingly slow to learn the lesson that the Assyrians, Persians, and Alexander the Great had all profited from in their conquest of Mesopotamia. True, the lesson was difficult to learn for generals who relied for victory on the invincibility of the Legion—5,000 superbly trained and disciplined men, each armed with two javelins, a sword, and a shield. But such heavily armed troops, so efficient in the European campaigns, were at a great disadvantage in the deserts of the Middle East, as the consul, M. Licinius Crassus, found to his cost at the Battle of Carrhae in 53 BC.

Crassus had crossed the Euphrates on to the Mesopotamian plain with seven legions and four cavalry squadrons, a total of 42,000 men. He had no camel-riders to reconnoitre what lay

[1] *Judges* 6: 3–5.

ahead. And what lay ahead were 10,000 Parthians, 1,000 of them camel-riders acting as scouts and carriers of weapons and water. The Roman legions found themselves drawn up in their traditional formation in the middle of the North Syrian plain, the infantry massed in close order in the centre, with a squadron, or wing, of cavalry on either flank. Crassus had opted for the traditional strategy and tactics: the enemy was to be crushed by sheer weight as the infantry, massed under the protection of their shields, moved inexorably forward, rank upon rank, until the enemy was literally submerged and either beaten down by the footmen or picked off by the cavalry. But the Parthians, most of whom were mounted on horses and camels, refused to play the Roman game. Instead, they began to ride around the flanks and rear of the infantry phalanx, firing a continuous shower of arrows and keeping up this barrage as the camel-trains brought in fresh supplies for the bowmen. The Romans began to split into isolated groups scattered about the desert, cut off from each other and the wells. At the end of the three-day battle, 20,000 of them were slain and 10,000 made prisoner. The Romans were never really ever again secure in their eastern provinces.

But the Parthian victory at Carrhae finally convinced the Roman commanders that a camel corps was essential. In AD 115, the emperor Trajan raised a regiment of *méharistes* in Syria, under the splendid title of *Ala I Ulpia Dromedariorum Milliaria*. The designation *Ala* (literally, a wing) shows that camels were now being used as cavalry, not just as baggage animals. And all along the foothills of Mesopotamia, in the Western and Eastern Deserts of Egypt, and as far south as the Sahara, *camelarii*, under the command of a Roman officer, patrolled the frontiers, protected the caravan trade, chastised the bandits, kept an eye on the wells, and carried dispatches to outlying forts. One can still trace these Roman frontier forts and still commemorate the names of camel-riders like the centurion Aurelius Calvisius Maximus, his standard-bearer

Hirraeus Malichus, and his lieutenant, Julius Paniscus. These men took their *goums* into the Arabian Desert east of the Nile, where the porphyry mines were worked by convicts, or into the Libyan Desert where other offenders (many of them Christians) were put to forced labour in the marble quarries.

It was the North African colony of Numidia, however, which needed an efficient camel corps perhaps more than any other province, as the French certainly found when their turn came to conquer and police this enormous wasteland. The Romans were not, of course, particularly interested in the interior of Africa, except as a supplier of ivory, slaves, and gold; but between AD 70 and 100, they decided to send two expeditions across the Sahara to discover something of what went on beyond the Numidian frontiers. The second of these expeditions was commanded by an officer called Julius Maternus. It started from Garama (the ancient capital of the Libyan Fezzan, today an abandoned oasis called Germa) and travelled southwards for four months in company with the King of the Garamantes, a powerful tribe from whom the Tuareg, or Veiled Men, may be directly descended. We do not know what place Julius's column reached, except that it was called Agisymba, 'a region of the Black Men where rhinoceroses abound', sufficient evidence to suggest that the Romans might actually have crossed the Sahara and reached the Niger river.

But the detachments of camel-riders which patrolled the frontiers in the last days of the Roman Empire were totally inadequate to repel the armies of the new Arabian prophet, Mohammed. In AD 642, Islamic troops launched a series of attacks from their base in Egypt, along the lines of oases in southern Cyrenaica and Tripolitania, penetrating into areas of the Sahara the Romans had never visited, let alone occupied. The heyday of the camel had arrived, and from now onwards events in all the desert regions bordering the civilized world were to be dominated by the camel. By the end of the sixteenth century, the Moroccan Sultan, Ahmad al-Mansur, 'the Golden', was able to send an army of some 6,000 men across 1,500 miles of the Sahara Desert from Marrakesh to Timbuctoo, an impossible feat without the 8,000 camels which accompanied the caravan.

Yet Western commanders throughout the first half of the nineteenth century remained deeply prejudiced against the camel as a war mount, so that those students of warfare who suggested the formation of 'camel brigades' were regarded with derision by professional soldiers. An American would as soon ride a donkey as a dromedary, as 'General' William Eaton was to find out on his ill-famed expedition 'to the shores of Tripoli'. Eaton had begun his intended invasion of Tripoli in March 1805 at the Arab's Tower near the Egyptian-Libyan border. His forces consisted of nine Americans, of whom six were 'private marines'; twenty-five cannoniers; thirty-eight Greeks; ninety bodyguards of the exiled Pasha Hamet Karamanli; a party of Arab horsemen; and 107 camels, together with 'a few asses'. Such a motley collection was lucky to get half-way to its destination before disintegrating; and the principal reason for the dissensions as well as the slowness of the invaders was the Americans' lack of familiarity with desert travel, though Eaton, who had been the US consul in Tunis for three years, should have known better. But as a result of his ignorance, he found himself involved in endless arguments about trifling details as to who was to ride the horses, how they were to be fed and watered in desert country, and so forth; whereas if he and his men had been mounted on camels, his army would have advanced thirty miles a day instead of twelve and a half.[1]

When the turn of the British and French came to conquer the old provinces of Asia and Africa, they displayed the same conservatism in their military tactics as the ancient Romans had shown. We find Napoleon's army in Egypt marching up the Nile in the formations used during the Austrian, Spanish, and

[1] Cornelius C. Felton, *Life of William Eaton*. The Library of American Biography. Boston: Hilliard Gray & Co, 1838.

Italian campaigns: the order of march was for the infantry to advance in squares with the artillery in between, the baggage in the centre, and the cavalry scouting ahead and on the flanks. The soldiers themselves, at the height of the Egyptian summer, were clad in thick serge coats, breeches and gaiters, and laden with rifles, packs, and rations consisting, of all things, of coarse biscuits. Apart from the uniforms, it might have been a Roman legion on the march through Northumberland. But the French very quickly learnt that not even their vastly superior discipline and fire-power could defeat the Bedouin tribesmen who, mounted on camels, harried the columns of tired and thirsty infantrymen, avoided pitched battles, and disappeared into the desert at will; and before the Egyptian campaign was over, Napoleon had incorporated into his army a regular camel corps. It was this squadron which finally caught up with and defeated his principal enemy, Murad Bey, near the oasis of Fayoum.

The British were to learn the same lesson in the Egyptian Sudan after the destruction of Hicks Pasha's army at El Obeid in Kordofan and the capture of Khartoum. Lord Wolseley's force ordered to relieve Gordon consisted of 14,000 British troops, but they moved much too slowly up the Nile in their flat-bottomed boats, despite the services of 380 Canadian and Red Indian *voyageurs*, to arrive in time to save the besieged garrison, and they had to turn back long before reaching Khartoum. The only column apparently capable of making speedy contact with Gordon was a brigade of the newly formed Camel Corps commanded by General Sir Herbert Stewart, which had to strike south across the 300 miles of the Bayuda Desert to reach Khartoum. Stewart's error was to include horses and infantrymen in such a column, for by the time it reached the wells at Abou Klea, both the horses and the men of foot were exhausted. They were ambushed and attacked by the Dervishes at the wells; the square broke; and, as the contemporary report puts it, 'only the camels, by checking the onward rush of the Arabs, saved the day; the English rallied and the square was reformed.' The column pushed on again, arrived at the banks of the Nile, abandoned their camels, and attempted to reach Khartoum aboard two river steamers. This was the second mistake. The steamers, plodding upstream against the current, were easy targets for the Dervish riflemen on the banks and had eventually to turn back. By then Khartoum had fallen and Gordon was dead. He might have been saved if General Stewart's Camel Corps had made straight for the city, unencumbered by the horses of the 19th Hussars and the 35th Sussex Regiment.

But both the French in Algeria and the British in Egypt were learning the lessons of desert warfare, albeit slowly. The French conquest of Algeria, for instance, was a particularly protracted and costly affair, involving heavy losses in men, pack animals, and material in skirmishes against ill-armed, undisciplined, but highly mobile camel-riders. The British in Egypt and the Sudan fared no better until Sir H. H. Kitchener incorporated camel cavalry and camel transport into his command. After the conquest of the Sudan, he used camel-riders to patrol and police the desert. At about the same time, the French with their eyes on the Sahara organized the famous *Compagnies Sahariennes*, led by their most brilliant officer, Marie Joseph François Henri Laperrine. The élite of these companies were the camel-riders, or *méharistes*, who, though few in number, eventually conquered the Sahara, not by seeking pitched battles, which was the conventional military strategy in Europe, but rather by avoiding them. Travelling fast, in small detachments of twenty or less, the camel-riders crossed and recrossed the desert in all seasons of the year, visited the most remote oases, made friends with the natives, protected their palmeries and their caravans, administered justice, and within ten years had joined North Africa with West Africa, making it possible to cross the desert in safety.

One of Laperrine's *méharistes* was Lieutenant Cortier, second-in-command of the Fourth Company of the Second Senegalese, the *goum* assigned to escort the Taodeni salt caravan which intelligence reports indicated was to be ambushed on the trail after leaving Timbuctoo.

Lieutenant Cortier's *goum* consisted of seven European officers and NCO's, 100 riflemen, and 160 camels. The caravan left Timbuctoo at the beginning of March 1904. They travelled north, camping at the wells around which were assembled the usual collection of mud huts and a turretted *ksar*, or fortress. As they progressed northwards, the desert became increasingly lifeless and the wells further apart. The shafts also became deeper, some of them over 300 feet deep. Down into these wells the caravaners had to lower their goat-skins and haul up enough brackish water to quench the thirst of thousands of men and animals. As the distance between the wells increased, water and fodder had to be carried on the backs of the camels. The terrible fear now, as the *goum* and caravan left the wells of Araouan, was that the next wells, 240 miles to the north at Bir Ounan, might be dry or occupied by bandits.

The decision was now made to march sixteen hours a day, non-stop, halting between the hours of 9 a.m. and 5 p.m. to rest. No one who has not made these long caravan *étapes* can imagine the physical fatigue and mental discomfort of sixteen hours' riding and walking under these conditions for day after day. Sixteen hours would put the *goum* some fifty miles along the road to the next well, as long as the camels could keep up their average speed. In contrast, the couriers who kept the outward-bound *goum* in touch with headquarters at Timbuctoo would travel 150 miles in twenty hours, or nearly eight miles an hour as opposed to three. The couriers, of course, rode thoroughbred *meharis*, while the military caravan escort used animals chosen for their strength and endurance.

On the third day out from the wells of Araouan, the *goum*

camped at a place famous for having the last few tufts of camel grass, after which there was not a single plant for over 300 miles. The camel men now collected every clump of grass and every bush they could find and tied it together in huge bundles which were loaded on to the camels. The unhappy animals had their mouths tightly lashed up so that they could not indulge in their favourite and only pleasure, ruminating, the theory of the Arabs being that if the creature could not chew the cud, the food he had eaten would digest more slowly and so sustain him longer. Hence the luckless camels could expect to stay gagged, breathing with difficulty, for perhaps as long as twenty-five days.

On 6 May, seven days after leaving the wells of Araouan, the *goum* reached Bir Ounan, worn with fatigue, since the only rest they had had for eight days was the halt after the night's march when they lay on the ground under the blazing sun, getting what shade they could from the camels. But on reaching the well at Ounan, they found only a trickle of water at the bottom of the shaft. They had to draw up this water all one day and night in order to provide about 500 litres, or 250 gallons, for their immediate needs and a reserve necessary to reach the next wells at Taodeni itself. Here, at the salt mines, they were supposed to meet another detachment commanded by Colonel Laperrine, who was transversing the dreaded Tanezrouft desert from southern Algeria.

But Laperrine did not arrive on the day he was due, nor for seven days thereafter, at which point the company from Timbuctoo had to start the return journey, as they were getting short of provisions. One section took the direct route by which they had come; the other, a new and longer, but allegedly easier route to the east of the main caravan track. Along this new and unexplored road, Lieutenant Cortier's camel-riders at last saw Laperrine's *méharistes* topping the crest of a dune. The subsequent scene of the advance scouts sounding their trumpets and of the French officers finally meeting

The Algiers slave market, where both black and white captives were exhibited for sale, in the early nineteenth century

Marco Polo of Cathay

Lawrence of Arabia

The Explorers

Gordon Laing of Timbuctoo

Aurel Stein of Central Asia

and embracing in the empty desert might have been shot for Hollywood.

The remainder of Lieutenant Cortier's story, after Colonel Laperrine had gone north to Taodeni and the Timbuctoo detachment had turned south again, is a grim record of a journey that was almost the last desert crossing for all of them. For three days after their departure, their guide was lost in the dunes. By the fourth day they were nearly out of water, and the temperature was 50° Centigrade in the shade. On the fifth day their water was gone; there was not a drop left except in the skins of the guide Sergeant Ribbe and two camel-drivers were sent ahead in the desperate hope of reaching the next well and returning with enough water to save the others from dying of thirst. The rest of the company followed their tracks with their dying camels, two of which were killed, the blackish water taken from their stomachs, and their blood used by the blacks to plaster on their heads. When the men could produce any urine, this, too, was drunk.

On the sixth day, two of the company fell unconscious and were left behind. The rest crawled along, still following the tracks of the advance party, as they had no other alternative. Then, on the seventh day, just as the sun was climbing the sky to the intolerable zenith and the soldiers, officers and men, knew that they were near the end, Sergeant Ribbe was seen coming out of the haze. He had found the well without the help of the Arab guide, who had begun to wander first to the north, then the south. Riding all that night, the sergeant had returned with just enough water to give his comrades the strength to go back for the two men who had been left, and then for the whole company to plod on to the well of Inichaig, where they arrived, says Lieutenant Cortier, 'in an indescribable state of weakness and fatigue'. Fortunately the well, situated in the midst of a vast plain, was only forty feet deep and full of sweet water.

Lieutenant Cortier got his men back to Timbuctoo, and the

great salt caravan returned from the Taodeni mines without being ambushed. Three of the French officer's men, however, did not survive the ordeal: two native camel-riders died of exhaustion, and the French sergeant, Mille, contracted amoebic dysentery and died on arriving in hospital. These were the kind of men who were later to be accused of imperialism, though the native caravaners who reached their journey's end in safety thanks to the military escort would not have thought of them in these terms. Nor did the French officers like Laperrine and Cortier think of themselves as either imperialists or racialists, since their desert patrols were made up of men prepared to endure the dangers and discomforts of caravan travel irrespective of whether they were white Frenchmen, brown Berbers, or black Africans.

By the end of the nineteenth century, the camel corps was an integral part of the French colonial army, with a special *mystique* which had belonged to the cavalry in older wars. The British, too, had developed a similar force of desert camel-riders for police duty in the Egyptian Sudan, for it was now recognized by even the most conservative military thinkers that the peace and security of the caravan routes were most efficiently maintained by small companies of men who accepted the hard routine of desert life and lived as the people of the sands lived, riding the same mounts, eating the same food, and wearing the same clothes. The *méharistes* ceased to be hated as occupation troops.

Finally, in the First World War, Lawrence of Arabia gave the camel cavalry a special glamour, for he appeared on the scene when the world was sickened with the mindless and mechanical slaughter on the static European battlefields. The image of the romantic Englishman charging through the desert on his white camel, the burning sun overhead by day, the glittering stars by night, was the stuff myths are made of. At last, when it was about to be phased out of warfare altogether, the camel was assured a place in military history—or, at least, in the popular conception of it. Soldiers like Laperrine of the Sahara and Lawrence of Arabia were part of the last chapter of a saga which had begun long before the rise of Babylon, to end some 3,000 years later with the Second World War.

A footnote to what was to be the final appearance of camel cavalry on the battlefield was written for me down on the shores of the Tunisian salt lake called the Chott Djerid in December 1943. Here, on the edge of the Sahara, a *goum* of tribesmen command by French officers had been stationed on the southern flank of the Allies' North African front with the assignment of containing a threatened German thrust across the Chott. If the Germans had attacked, they would have done so with tanks, and the *goum*, one assumes, would have been annihilated in a matter of minutes. But all was peaceful along the lake. The camels were kneeling, placidly chewing the cud with their usual contemptuous expression; the camel-men were preparing their evening meal on little fires of twigs; the French officers, beautifully cloaked and sandalled, were reclining under a palm tree which sloped at exactly the right angle for a movie shot. Soon the enormous stars of a Saharan night lit up the heavens. It was difficult to believe that somewhere across the lake squatted a squadron of German Tiger tanks, sixty tons in weight and armed with 88 mm guns and hard to imagine what we would have done if the snout of one of them had suddenly appeared atop a dune. It was, in its way, a bizarre scene in the middle of a modern war, though no more bizarre than if, in some future war, those same Tiger tanks were to undertake to defend us against hydrogen bombs fired from satellites. It merely demonstrated that the camel cavalry had had its day, along with the Light Brigades of the nineteenth century and the Mongol horsemen of Genghis Khan. Tanks will no doubt have theirs.

The Camel Caravans
of America and Australia

The last chapter in the long history of desert transport occurs in two very unlikely places—in the United States, where just over a century ago camel caravans were crossing the wastelands of the south-west, and in the empty vastness of central Australia. In Australia, the camels were highly successful, and, being able to survive in country that would not support a goat, made possible crossings and exploration of the dreaded Red Desert and the building of roads, railways, and the Overland Telegraph line. In America, caravans followed trails from the Gulf of Mexico to the Pacific, from the Rio Grande to Mexico City, and worked mountain tracks leading from the gold, silver, and salt mines in the west and south. That they did not survive like the great Saharan *azalais* is not as surprising as that they existed at all. They are, indeed, a very strange, forgotten chapter of American history.

The introduction of the camel into the United States began as a military and commercial project, though some would describe it as a political stunt. At all events, in 1855 the United States Congress appropriated $30,000 (worth probably about ten times as much today) to import camels into the US for use as cavalry patrols and freight-carriers in the desert country of the south-west. The scheme was not exactly popular, either with Congress, the army, or the general public, for the camel was a very alien creature to Americans, even though the New World seems to have been its primeval home. Still, Secretary Jefferson Davis's plan was approved, and by 1856 the first consignment of thirty-four camels was landed at Powder Horn,

Texas—one of them, a Tunisian camel called Mahomet, having been at sea for over nine months. The camels celebrated their joy at finding firm ground under their feet by rearing, kicking, fighting, bellowing, and eating their way through the fences of prickly pear which the army quartermaster had imagined would keep them inside the corral.

All this did not endear the camels to their keepers, and within a few months several had been beaten to death, including the most valuable, a gentle she-camel from Smyrna. Some were knifed in the ribs, some shot as 'ghosts' glimpsed in the fog, and some deliberately left to die in heavy mud, which is the one type of terrain the camel cannot cope with. It appears that most Americans of the time found the new arrivals either frightening or ludicrous, and the cameleer who went ahead of them shouting, 'Get out of the way. The camels are coming', was not a popular official. It was widely reported in the press, and highly exaggerated in the taverns, that the camels caused horses, mules, cattle, dogs, and domestic animals in general to run amok, while their smell and, more particularly, their disdainful regard, offended the backwoodsmen out West whither the camels were bound. It is no wonder that in such uncongenial surroundings some of the animals just knelt down and died in a manner not uncharacteristic of this strange, remote creature, while every pregnant female produced a dead calf, with the exception of Rosie who, though not even suspected of being gravid, gave birth on the trail. None of the drivers knew enough about camels to place the baby in a sling on his mother's back, as the Bedouin do, so that when the day's march was done, he could be suckled and cared for. This little camel was left to die on the road.

Yet there were a few influential Americans who were real enthusiasts for camels as both cavalry and caravaners. Jefferson Davis, for instance, seems to have been prompted by his desire to unite the southern states with the newly-acquired Spanish-speaking south-west, so as to form a strong political, economic, and cultural *bloc* in opposition to the Yankee north. Union over this vast, as yet unexplored and unsettled, territory would depend, of course, on connecting roads and trails; and since much of the terrain of Texas, New Mexico, Arizona, and California was desert, Davis got it into his head that the camel was the best beast for both the job of patrolling the wastelands and that of transporting freight from the ports of the Gulf of Mexico to the townships along the Pacific coast. It would almost seem as though the Secretary of War had had some personal experience of camels and caravans in the Sahara or Arabian deserts. In actual fact, he had never travelled farther west than Cuba and had never seen a camel in his life.

Though his plan to buy camels in Africa and Asia Minor and ship them back to the States at first excited the derision of the Congress, the money was voted, and a naval vessel was put at the disposal of Major Henry Constantine Wayne, who was ordered to 'proceed without delay to the Levant, stopping on the way in London and Paris to find out what he could about camels'.

With the exception of a few army officers, the English and French knew no more about camels than the Americans, though they were very polite and willingly showed the Americans the two or three animals housed in their zoos. The French had one, the British two, but the London keeper admitted that he knew nothing about camels since his pair had never been ill and never did anything but stand about and be stared at by the public. Major Wayne and his team had to wait until they reached Africa to discover what camels were really like.

Their first lesson was in a camel-market in Tunis where every inhabitant, including the children, knew that two Americans (equals two millionaires) were offering to buy camels, price no object. Camels of every age and condition were rounded up for miles around, and driven to Tunis as fast as their legs would carry them, until Major Wayne and his navy colleague Lieutenant Porter, USN, fled back to their ship, after purchasing one camel 'at great personal sacrifice', according to its owner. The Americans were about to sail away from Tunis, which was now practically overrun with camels, when a couple more appeared on the dockside, gifts from the Bey of Tunis and therefore not to be refused. Major Wayne wondered how he was going to get one camel, let alone three, aboard his ship. But this was eventually accomplished by means of pullings, pushings, blocks, tackles, and blows. One of the camels thus embarked aboard the American vessel was that same Mahomet who was not to disembark until nine months later.

The Wayne mission now sailed east to Smyrna, where the US consul had been doing some research into the availability of camels via Middle Eastern missionaries. The missionaries were not interested in camels and not amused by the consul's questionnaire. 'No time to bother about camels,' one replies: 'too busy writing epitaphs for gravestones.' Another in the Trebizond region notes: 'No camels here. Same goes for storks, magpies and buffaloes.' Yet there were evidently plenty of camels in and around the Levant, and a Turk, on hearing that there were none in the US, condoled with the Americans for being so lamentably behind the times in the field of transportation.

But the major and his colleagues were learning fast, for after leaving Smyrna and continuing their search for camels in Egypt, they had at least learnt what animals to avoid: camels which had been cauterized on the belly or chest, indicating that these beasts had suffered some internal injury; camels with bald patches (due to the application of hot tar), which were suffering from the itch, or scurvy; camels living in the towns and villages, which were invariably mangy, half-starved, ill-treated, and broken in spirit. Good camels came from the studs of rich breeders like the sultan; or from the Bedouin Arabs, who were the only people to treat their camels humanely.

At the end of several months' negotiations, Major Wayne had acquired 34 camels, nine of them *mehari*, or trotting camels; twenty baggage camels; two Bactrian sires and Arabian dromedary dams; and a young male Arabian. The camels were stalled aboard the American ship when she left Alexandria. Seven calves were born during the voyage, which was beset by gales both in the Mediterranean and the Atlantic. Only two of these babies survived long enough to reach Texas, where they died shortly after landing.

Those Americans who had been enthusiastic for the idea of a camel cavalry and camel caravans were highly gratified that the project had got under way so successfully, and the supply ship which had brought the first contingent was immediately dispatched back to the Mediterranean to pick up another load, along with some professional camel-men. Some of these men, notably the Syrian Hadji Ali, whose name quickly became Americanized into 'Hi Jolly', were to gain a sort of notoriety during the short lifetime of the US camel cavalry; and the *haj's* tomb, with suitable inscription, is today something of a tourist attraction at Quartzsite, Arizona.[1]

Forty-four more excellent camels were shipped from Constantinople on the second trip, of which forty-one were still alive when the ship reached the mouth of the Mississippi in January 1857. These were now added to the original thirty-four camels, thus giving a total of seventy-five camels, property of the US Government and the newest arm of the US Army.

Major Wayne, who by this time had become something of an expert, believed that the camels would be more suitable for the second of their assignments: namely, as pack animals. Moreover, he had become intrigued with camels and wanted to breed them with the same care and attention devoted to the breeding of thoroughbred horses, though his enthusiasm for

---

[1] The epitaph reads: *The Last Camp of Hi Jolly, born somewhere in Syria about 1828, died at Quartzsite Dec 16, 1923. Came to this country Feb 10, 1856. Camel Driver, Packer, Scout. Over 30 years a faithful aid to the US Government.*

his camels was not shared by either his fellow-soldiers or the general public. He wrote to Jefferson Davis's successor, the new Secretary of War John B. Floyd, that 'the prejudices, fears, and objections of all classes are to be met only by successful demonstration'. Asked by the Secretary what sort of demonstration, he suggested an expedition to survey a wagon road across the desert country between Fort Defiance in New Mexico and Fort Tejon in California. Wayne himself did not get the job of leading this expedition, which was entrusted to a naval officer on the grounds that desert travel was, after all, very similar to that of ocean voyaging. The choice was Lieutenant Edward Fitzgerald Beale, USN, as leader of the Wagon Road Expedition of 1857; it was fortunate that he was an enthusiast about camels and delighted to lead the expedition. No sooner had the contingent of twenty-five been assembled at San Antonio, Texas, than the cameleers—Syrians, Greeks, and Turks, who had been brought over with the camels—refused to go on the journey on the grounds that they had not been paid their salary of $15 a month for six months. Beale, however, seems to have sorted this out, and several of the cameleers, Hi Jolly among them, marched with the caravan.

Edward Beale proved himself a worthy companion of the great explorers of the nineteenth century—men of great bravery, intelligence, and modesty. And though he belonged to that special breed of adventurer who was then roaming about Mexico and the newly-acquired states of the southwest—soldiers, scouts, trappers, prospectors, and gold-miners—he was, and always remained, a gentleman with a gentleman's sympathy for the weak and oppressed. The mules were treated humanely; the dogs were allowed to ride in the wagons when they became footsore; and the camels were never forced to march faster than their natural speed of three miles per hour. Beale discovered that the dromedary was a most docile beast, even though 'with all its gentleness it has a most

ferocious-looking set of teeth, which it displays with a roar
rivalling that of the royal Bengal tiger.' The American knew
what the majority of African and Asian camel drivers are
ignorant of, or, more likely, indifferent to: that the camel's
hump is extremely sensitive and easily bruised by an ill-fitting
saddle. Beale did what he could to alleviate the animal's
discomfort, and was eventually rewarded with a collection of
docile and patient beasts to whom he became more and more
attached, as his journal reveals if one reads between the lines
of the following entry:

As our lines of wagons ascended the hill, the camels appeared
on the further side, winding down the steep road, and made
a picture well worthy the pen of a great artist. The steep,
grey rocks, the beautiful green bottom, or meadow, the
clear sparkling stream, the loose animals, the wagons and
teams, and then old Mahomet [the Tunisian camel], with
the long line of his grave and patient followers, winding
cautiously, picking step by step their way down the road on
the opposite side, was a very interesting and beautiful
scene.[1]

Anyone who has travelled with camels in, for instance, the
Hoggar or Air Mountains, recognizes the accuracy of this
description and feels instinctively that the writer was strongly
attached to 'old Mahomet . . . and his grave and patient
followers'. Beale insisted in his report to the Secretary of War
at the end of the expedition that if more camels were to be
imported, a corps of Mexicans should be trained to care for
them since:

The Americans of the class who seek such employment are

---

[1] *Uncle Sam's Camels*. The journals of Lt Edward Fitzgerald Beale and May
Humphreys Stacey, ed. by L. B. Lesley. Cambridge, Mass; Harvard UP, 1929,
p 135.

totally unfit for it, being for the most part harsh, cruel, and impatient with animals entrusted to their care.[1]

Of course, most Americans were almost totally ignorant of the camel and his ways, so that even those who had had an opportunity of seeing the animals at work continued to make fantastic mistakes concerning their size and capabilities, as this item from the 21 July 1858 issue of the *Los Angeles Star* reveals:

> Camels, eight in number, came into town from Fort Tejon after provisions for that camp. The largest ones pack a ton and can travel sixteen miles an hour.

Beale's Wagon Route Survey officially ended near Zuni, New Mexico on 21 February 1858. On this date Beale ended his journal on a solemn but lyrical note:

> A year in the wilderness ended! During this time I have conducted my party from the Gulf of Mexico to the shores of the Pacific Ocean, and back again to the eastern terminus of the road, through a country for the most part entirely unknown, and inhabited by hostile Indians, without the loss of a man. I have tested the value of camels, marked a new road to the Pacific, and travelled 4,000 miles without an accident.[2]

His verdict on the value of camels was again almost lyrical; for he grew not only proud of his charges, but extremely fond of them, as this passage in the report he submitted to John B. Floyd, the Secretary of War, shows:

> My admiration for the camels increases daily with my experience of them. The harder the test they are put to the

[1] *Ibid*, p 184.
[2] *Op cit*, p 124.

more fully they seem to justify all that can be said of them. They pack water for others four days under a hot sun and never get a drop; they pack heavy burdens of corn and oats for months and never get a grain; and on the bitter grease-wood and other worthless shrubs not only subsist but keep fat; withal, they are so perfectly docile and so admirably contented with whatever fate befalls them. No one could do justice to their merits or value in expeditions of this kind, and I look forward to the day when every mail route across this continent will be conducted and worked altogether with this economical and noble brute.[1]

Yet it was inevitable that Davis's experiment should fail. The scheme was manifestly impractical and, in some respects, plainly ridiculous. The United States of the mid-nineteenth century when the continent was being criss-crossed with railroads needed camels to carry freight about as urgently as it needed elephants to haul logs. However, nothing much was lost; the experiment had cost the tax-payer only a few thousand dollars, and a lot of people had obtained a deal of instruction and entertainment from 'old Mahomet' and his companions. The camels themselves had certainly earned their keep and under humane masters like Major Wayne and Lieutenant Beale had enjoyed a few years of agreeable camel-line existence.

But the end was inevitable, and it was hastened by the outbreak of the war between the States. Public interest in the camels evaporated as the fearsome struggle continued, and there was nobody left in the Government who had the inclination, let alone the time, to bother with a herd of strange animals wandering about somewhere in New Mexico. Out on the Pacific coast, which was a region divided culturally as well as geographically from the East, camels were still 'news', especially as some entrepreneur was importing them from

[1] *Ibid*, p 233.

Manchuria. Fifteen Mongolian Bactrians—the survivors of a group of thirty-two that had been taken aboard at Vladivostok—were landed at San Francisco in 1859. In the style of the journalism of the period, a reporter of the *San Francisco Daily Evening Bulletin* [sic] proclaimed that these beasts were 'to bend the uninhabitable frontier of the continent into contact and annihilate the wilderness that separates the new from the old West'.

What the Asian camels were actually used for was to carry salt 200 miles from a marsh, or sink, in south-western Nevada to a mill at Lake Washoe, twenty miles south of Reno, Nevada. The camels carried their loads with the immense patience Lieutenant Beale found so appealing, but they were despised by their drovers, who no more entertained the idea of grooming them than they did of petting them. A visitor who saw those Bactrians that managed to survive the Nevada salt trail and were then used to carry ore from an Arizona mine, states that so much salt and alkali had accumulated in the long hair of their humps that 'great loathsome sores covered the area touched by the saddle.' In addition, their great soft pads had been so split and injured by the rough ground that they had become unserviceable and were either killed or turned loose. A second batch of Bactrians which had been imported from China about this time were fitted with leather shoes before being sent on the Cariboo Road in British Columbia. This experiment, too, was a failure, and for the usual reasons: the camels were grossly overloaded, maltreated, and despised. After a year the caravan was discontinued, and the hated camels were driven off into the mountains of the Canadian province to survive with the last of the big-horn sheep, the Rocky Mountain goat, the grizzly bear, the moose, and the woodland caribou.

In the meantime, the Government-owned camels which Major Wayne had so enthusiastically nurtured and Lieutenant Beale had so successfully employed were scattered about in different camps, and nobody in authority seemed to know what to do with them. It was no longer even clear who owned the camels, since the herd of some eighty which had been kept at Camp Verde in Texas and which belonged to the Federal Government in January 1861 became the property of the Confederates the following month, when the Yankee camp surrendered. The Confederates were far too preoccupied to bother about the militarily useless animals, which appear to have been turned over to local boys to do with as they liked. The Texan youths seemed to regard the slow-moving prehistoric-looking beasts as targets for amusement or malice: so we hear of one camel being knifed to death; another being shoved over a cliff for the hell of it; and others being allowed to escape into the wilds.

By the end of the war, the Federal Government, confronted with the enormous problems of reconstruction, was anxious to get rid of the animals which were now turning up all over the place, from Texas to Iowa. It appears that both the Federal and the Confederate soldiers had periodically amused themselves by hunting down loose camels in the wilder regions of Texas, New Mexico, and Arizona, and it was from this period, between 1860 and 1890, that the legends of 'wild camels' were born and grew to the usual absurd proportions, nourished by those writers who specialize in exploiting popular myths. Thus we have the 'Great Red Camel', or the 'Old White Camel'; the camel with an antique army saddle on its back; the camel ridden by a gibbering skeleton; and the camel following the crazed goldminer, its saddle-bags loaded with gleaming nuggets.

Of the camels that remained, some were sold to Ringling Brothers' Circus, while others became the property of a certain 'Colonel' Bethel Coopwood, who set up a short-lived caravan from Laredo, Texas to Mexico City. By 1890 there were no more working camels left in the United States, except the specimens exhibited in circuses and zoos. And by 1900 there were certainly no free or 'wild' camels left either, for the several score which had escaped or been driven into the desert, had either been shot for fun, captured and sold to zoos, or killed and eaten by the Indians. It was symptomatic of how scarce game was getting by this time that the Red men were glad to eat camel which, as anyone who has tried it knows, has the taste and consistency of an old bicycle tyre.

No one, now that the original enthusiasts were either dead or confined to their rocking-chairs, regretted the disappearance of this exotic beast from the scene, for the camel never really 'belonged' on the American continent, any more than it did on the continent of Europe. The age of steam and rail made it obsolete. The terminal date for the American camels and the caravan trails they opened up is 27 April 1934, when the following news item was published in the *Oakland Tribune*:

> Topsy, the last survivor of the camel herds that trekked across the desert of Arizona and California, is dead. Attendants at Griffith Park here destroyed her after she became crippled with paralysis in the park lot where she spent the declining years of her life. Before she was brought to Griffith Park, Topsy was one of the camels that were abandoned to live in a wild state on the Arizona desert.

Australians began introducing camels into their territories at about the same time as the Americans, and for the same purpose. Around the middle of the last century, the idea was to try out the camel as a pack carrier in the roadless regions of both continents. But whereas enthusiasm for the experiment was on the whole markedly lacking in the US, the many reports by Australians on the subject, in addition to constituting a well-documented and important chapter of their social and economic history, emphasize the value of the camel as a vital factor in the development of their nation. Further, this much maligned animal is treated by the authors with a sympathy which is unusual among Anglo-Saxons. Australian camels have names and personalities, as they do in Arab countries. The bull, Robin, leader of missionary Robert Plowman's caravan in 1912, is described as 'very steady, very strong, and a good walker'; Doctor, 'about nine feet tall, deep in the barrel, broad in the chest, and massively built'; and Shah, 'the clown of the team'.

Camels in the Outback not only had names, but were regarded with affection and treated accordingly. Australians seem not to have suffered from the prejudice which has been characteristic of English and American opinion ever since the *Encyclopaedia Britannica* (Eleventh Edition), quoting Sir Francis Palgrave, described the camel as 'from first to last an undomesticated and savage animal rendered serviceable by stupidity alone'.[1] Such aspersions certainly did not prevent Australians from importing and breeding camels from the 1840s until the 1900s, when there were over 6,000 of them working in the interior, with an unknown number living wild in the Outback. Moreover, all those who had any actual experience of camels held the contrary view—Herbert Barker, an Australian cameleer, for instance says that 'a camel is one of the nicest animals there is, and yet he is continually persecuted by writers.'

So just when the Americans were deciding that the camel and the camel caravan were not the solution to their problems, the Australians were coming more and more to depend upon this animal to open up the wastelands which neither men nor horses had been able to conquer during the first century of the continent's colonization. In fact, this lesson had been learnt as early as 1844, when Sir Roderick Murchison had pointed out to the leading geographers of the time that the

---

[1] Sir Francis could have known no more about camels than he did about kangaroos, since he apparently seldom set foot outside England and had certainly never seen a camel in his life. His son, William Gifford, the diplomatist, did cross Central Asia with a caravan in 1862; was therefore familiar with 'the ship of the desert'; and may have been the author of this fiction.

The Sahara is littered with the forts of invaders.
Above: A castle of the Garamantes, allies of the Romans.
Below: A Turkish fort in the Fezzan

The oasis of Ghadames, the Roman fortress-city of Cydamus, vestiges of which still survive. *Below*: The totally abandoned town of Djado on the Chad-Mourzouk-Tripoli Slave Road

exploration of the centre of Australia was virtually impossible without the aid of camels.

The camel first appeared on the scene on 29 July 1846, when a young English settler set out to explore the unknown country of the salt lakes north of Port Augusta, South Australia. John Ainsworth Horrocks's party included four white companions, an Aboriginal, five horses, a cart, and the only camel in Australia. Horrocks himself rode the camel. The explorer was representative of that special breed of Australian pioneers who opened up the arid wasteland of the Outback; and his dromedary was the prototype of thousands of camels which later contributed to the initial development of Australia.

It is perhaps significant that Horrocks died on his journey, for this was the penalty that many subsequent explorers of the 'Red Centre' were to pay for their ventures into the unknown. The first two travellers to cross the continent from south to north, Burke and Wills, killed their last exhausted camel in the marshes of Coopers Creek in a final, desperate attempt to survive. So, too, other camels were to die in their hundreds to make possible the crossing of the Centre, and the building of roads, railways, and telegraph lines, without which Australia would still remain a group of isolated states. These curious and aloof animals made possible the exploration and exploitation of the continent for over half a century.

By 1872, when the first crossing of Western Australia had finally been achieved, the leader of the expedition, Colonel Egerton Warburton, was able to assert that no horses would have survived the journey, nor would any member of the party, without the caravan of seventeen camels with which he started from Alice Springs.[1] 'I have often abused camels,' he writes in his diary: 'I will never do so again.' His contemporary, Ernest Giles, who twice crossed the continent on his expeditions of 1872 and 1876, came to exactly the same conclusion:

[1] Peter Egerton Warburton, *Journey Across the Western Interior of Australia*. Sampson, Low: London, 1875, p 142.

12

To a man accustomed to camels for exploration, the beautiful horse sinks into the insignificance of a pygmy when compared to his majestic rival, the mighty ship of the desert; and assuredly if it had not been for these creatures and their marvellous powers, I never could have performed the three last journeys which complete my public explorations in Australia.[1]

By the 1880s, the camel had proved superior to the horse, not only for exploration, but for carrying freight in the Outback. It was more in demand than either horses or bullocks in many desert regions, and caravans were now passing between isolated outposts as regularly as they were between the Libyan oases. These caravans were, of course, small, and there were never any *azalais* the size of the great Saharan salt caravans, which sometimes consisted of 20,000 camels and their attendant cameleers. The largest Australian caravan consisted of a string of some eighty animals, owned and worked by an Afghan and his Aboriginal 'boy'. The Afghans, or 'ghans', as the Australians soon called them, had come over with the camels imported from Peshawar, and the men themselves were Pakistani—not Afghans at all. They remained a wholly alien, though not rejected, community, living in their own shanty towns, true nomads with no possessions that could not be transported on the back of a camel, and covering in their travels about three-quarters of the continent. They ran their caravans to all those towns and stations which were beyond the reach of horse and bullock wagons, hundreds of their camels taking in supplies to the sheep stations and the copper and gold mines, and bringing out wool and ore to the railheads. They were much in demand by dealers in spirits, since as Mohammedans they did not drink themselves and could consequently be trusted to deliver a consignment of whisky or rum to a mining camp intact. The

[1] Ernest Giles, *Australia Twice Traversed*. London: Sampson, Low, 1889 Vol 2, p 342.

principal Afghan caravan centres were Alice Springs in the Northern Territory, Broken Hill in New South Wales, Maree in South Australia, and Birdsville in Queensland—settlements comparable with the shanty towns of the American 'Wild West'.

Seeing that caravanning was highly profitable, a number of white Australians attempted to set up business in competition with the Afghans. But they soon discovered that they had a great deal to unlearn as well as to learn. It is not easy for men who have been brought up with horses to establish a rapport with camels, whose attributes are quite different; and the white drovers who decided to profit from the growing caravan trade had little success in the use of the camel as a pack animal. The techniques of training and working these dromedaries were clearly a monopoly of the Afghans. On the other hand, it was native Australians who first trained camels to pull wagons in teams, sometimes as many as eighteen camels to a wagon, something no Asiatic or African camel-man had ever attempted. The arrangement was to place three camels between the shafts and five sets of three in front of these 'shafters'. A wagon thus harnessed would be loaded with anything up to twenty tons of freight, and it was the camel-teamster's boast that his animals could pull more and better than horses. Certainly in sandy terrain the camel was admitted to be a superior hauler to all other draft animals, the donkey coming second, the horse third, and the bullock fourth.

In consequence of his usefulness, the camel soon became so familiar a feature of the Australian interior that the arrival of a caravan at a cattle station was as normal as it was in a Saharan oasis. Camels pulled the settlers' buggies, carried the mail, toted sleepers for the railroads then being built, and marched with thousands of telephone poles on their backs while the Overland Telegraph Line was being constructed in the Centre. This was the last great achievement in the modernization of the Dominion—the building in 1873-4 of a communications network consisting of 36,000 poles carrying a single strand of iron wire for 1,800 miles right through the heart of Australia, enabling the colony to communicate with Britain, the mother-land, in a matter of minutes instead of months. Adelaide, the capital of South Australia, was now linked with Darwin, the capital of the Northern Territory; Darwin with London and the rest of the world. Moreover, the dreaded 'Red Centre' had at last been penetrated, surveyed, and to some extent conquered. The sheep and cattle farmers now began moving their flocks and herds steadily northwards in search of new lands. Prospectors, then miners, moved in. Homesteads which became small towns were established all along the route of Overland Telegraph Line, and a water-hole, called Stuart by the construction gangs, had a hundred years later grown into a thriving town called Alice Springs.

As late as 1914, when the eastern end of the desert section of the Trans-continental Railway was being laid, camels still proved indispensable, as the advance camp of the workers could only be reached by caravan, and 210 camels were regularly in service across this 700 miles of waterless desert.

It was really the sheer efficiency of camels that persuaded the pastoralist Sir Thomas Elder to import and breed camels in 1862. Here was a pack animal that could carry up to seventeen hundredweight on its back, which was regularly transporting 600 lbs of wool, at eighteen miles per day for several days without water, and all that time feeding itself in desert country. For this reason the camel was still being extensively used in Australia for transport and freight as late as the third decade of the twentieth century, when the rest of the civilized world associated caravans only with the Sahara. It was really only the arrival on the scene of the 'cap and goggles' aviators of the 1920s which eventually led to the discontinuance of the little camel-trains kept on the road by the Afghans. But camels were still in service for special duties right up to the outbreak of the Second World War, when the explorer Cecil Madigan led a caravan across the Simpson desert, the first traverse ever made of that 90,000 square miles of dunes. Madigan's achievement represents the triumphant conclusion of an historical phase that began with John Horrocks's single camel in 1846.

But the day of this long-suffering beast of burden, which for over half a century had been as much part of the Australian desert landscape as it was of Arabia, was now over. This was due not only to the extension of the railways and the building of paved roads for automobiles (Australia having become the world's third most motorized nation, after the US and Canada), but to the advent of the aeroplane. The institution of a regular and reliable air service throughout the continent had been slow in coming, primarily because of the dangers of forced landings in the desert. But with the introduction of safe light aircraft, Australians became air-minded people, and the idea of the missionary wandering about with his camel caravan seemed incredible in the age of the Flying Doctor and his Cessna plane.

Yet it is still possible to see the descendants of the camels that carried Burke and Wills, Giles and Madigan, on their journeys into the Outback and still possible to talk to men who have travelled there with a camel caravan. But this chapter of history is fast becoming a memory to most Australians, and the dwellers in the great modern cities would find it difficult to believe that within their own lifetime camel-bells could be heard along the road to Alice Springs, as once they were heard on the road to Samarkand.

Epilogue

Those who have travelled with a camel caravan or have visited the remoter oases have seen the last vestiges of a system of trade and communication which has existed in some form or another for at least 6,000 years. But the continuity and longevity of the system offer no guarantees against progress: within the last century a number of caravan centres have disappeared altogether; others have been abandoned and others are dying as the population, having nothing productive to do, moves away.

This process is not, of course, new, as the number of formerly prosperous cities along the old caravan routes illustrates. The most spectacular of them are situated on the Silk and Incense Roads—Balkh in Afghanistan, Palmyra in Syria, Petra in Jordan. Other abandoned sites include mysterious ruins like Marib in the Yemen, Sijilmassa in Morocco, and Drigana in the southern Sahara. The very names and locations of others are still in question.

Some of the old caravan centres, though dead, have been preserved by some accident of climate, or the absence of a local population who would normally destroy an old town for its building material, as so many ancient cities, Babylon among them, have been destroyed. Djado in the Republic of Niger is such a place. Well supplied with water, Djado was able to accommodate large caravans by supplying them with dates, vegetables, meat, and guides for the journey south into the sand seas. As the oasis flourished, a large town of mud bricks was built on the main hillock, with look-out towers on the surrounding mounds, so that from afar Djado resembles a medieval Italian town perched on its hill, with the houses rising one above the other, bespeaking the narrow streets and squalid habitations which huddle together for security inside defensive walls. But a marsh, which breeds mosquitoes by the myriad, now surrounds the town: it is the result of the abandonment of the palmeries and gardens and the destruction of the irrigation system. In fact, everything at Djado is destroyed except the shell of the houses. The houses are empty and beginning to crumble, the streets are deserted, the entire place is now the abode of adders and scorpions. On the out-skirts of the town the palms have been cut down and many of the trunks have been burnt. The patches which were once gardens have been covered with sand. The wells have been filled in; all signs of human life and effort are absent; and a region which even today could still support a sizeable popula-tion is now as deserted and arid as the great Ténéré sand sea nearby. Djado takes its place with those other caravan centres—Antioch, Palmyra, Petra, and Marib.

What was its history? And what happened to it? It was probably first occupied and developed as early as the tenth century AD and abandoned about 1950 after the French had tried in vain to encourage the resettlement of the region. In fact, a French fort of classic Foreign Legion construction stands within a mile of the abandoned town, the fort, too, empty and slowly becoming engulfed by the sand dunes. Obviously Djado's chances of reviving are negligible, despite the abund-ance of water and the availablity of land for date palms and vegetable gardens. For the period in which the town flourished is as ancient history now as the age of prehistoric hunters who lived on the escarpment overlooking the oasis, hunters who left behind on the rocks under which they sheltered their strange drawings of antelopes and elephants and cattle and animals which have long since become extinct.

The decline of oases like Djado and the decrease of the

caravans have meant a profound social as well as economic change throughout Asia and Africa. It is ironic that would-be-benefactors who recommend the substitution of one truck for 200 camels, thus ameliorating (they believe) the woes of man and beast, far from improving the desert people's lot are destroying not only their means of livelihood but their very society. For once the camelline economy is upset, the traditional closely-knit life of the Sahara will be ended forever. It is with this in mind that a European observer who knew the desert speaks of the process of destroying the nomads with anger and, indeed, sadness:

> Here are a people perfectly adapted to the natural environment, not only physically through the sharpness of their senses, the sureness of their instincts, the speed of their reflexes, but also by their social organization and their sense of honour; and simply to obtain workmen for the oil fields, it is planned to transform these lordly people who command our respect by the dignity of their attitudes and the wisdom of their rare utterances, into a rabble seeking jobs and doles.[1]

This transformation of formerly free people into a mindless proletariat conditioned to do the will of a central government some thousand or so miles away from the oases is at present a slow if inevitable process, for the desert has always been a formidable opponent to every kind of would-be conqueror. Moreover, these vast wastelands have had to be ignored for the time being by their new rulers, even though such officials are usually eager to control, if not altogether abolish, all forms of nomadism, which they associate with hostility towards a centralized authoritarian régime. And this, of course, is the nub of the matter. The nomads who wander back and forth

[1] Robert Capot-Rey, 'The Present State of Nomadism in the Sahara', Arid-Zone Research: Vol 18, The Problems of the Arid Zone. UNESCO, 1962, p 307.

across frontiers in pursuit of the caravan trade do not regard themselves as beholden to politicians far away in the new glass-and-cement offices of government ministries. The camel-riders of the desert have little in common with the officials who ride in Mercedes limousines through the pot-holed streets of the capital cities. Yet it is these officials and the politicians who appoint them who are bent upon industrialization and urbanization, all in the name of progress, which usually means the imposition of Western ideas and, indeed, of Western values on primitive peoples. But to those who know the desert and its life, the disruption of the old way, hard and unrewarding though it is, means the destruction of the economic and social system of tens of thousands of people—their way of life, what they produce, how they produce it, and how they make use of their resources: in rearing camels, pasturing them, feeding the camel-men from the oasis gardens, and organizing the caravans to transport goods from one oasis to another, so that every desert-dweller, man, woman, and child, is interdependent within a balanced system.

Even so, the ancient way of the caravaners still survives and may survive for a few more decades, even in an age of faster-than-sound travel. And how curious an experience it is to be lying at night on the ground in the middle of the desert with no sound other than the gurglings of a ruminating camel nearby and to hear the hum of a jet aircraft passing somewhere 30,000 feet overhead, carrying people dressed in clean formal garments and looking forward to a shower in the next hotel, after travelling 5,000 miles in the time it takes the caravan to travel thirty—people utterly oblivious, not only of the men asleep on the sand below, but of the idea that such men exist at all.

But they do exist, though threatened with inevitable destruction. The nomads are still loading their camels with dates and millet and salt for transport to the far oases. At the oases the inhabitants still welcome them with jugs of cool water. At the wells the women are still filling their buckets; in the palmeries the men are still singing as they fertilize the date trees; and out in the open dunes a few of the world's most beautiful wild animals still survive—the gazelle, the addex, the fennec, and the desert lark. Such, still, is the world of the caravans.

Bibliography

The following bibliography has been compiled for readers who wish to investigate the history of the old caravan routes in greater detail. Unfortunately all the most informative books—especially the works of the nineteenth-century explorers—are out of print and hence only obtainable in national or university libraries. But though difficult to find, these old travellers' tales are well worth the effort of tracking down. Beautifully written and illustrated, they provide a fund of social and economic information which enables the historian today to understand the problems of the undeveloped regions of Africa and Asia, particularly the urgent problem of what is to become of the oases, caravans, and desert communities.

The Incense Road

ALBRIGHT, WILLIAM FOZWELL, *Exploring Sinai*, Baltimore: Reprinted from the Bulletin of the American Schools of Oriental Research, 1948

ARNAUD, THOMAS J., 'Pièces relatifs aux inscriptions himyarites', *Journal Asiatique*, vol V (1845)

ATCHLEY, E. G. C. F., *A History of the Use of Incense in Divine Worship*, Alcuin Club Collection, London: Longmans, 1909

BENT, JAMES THEODORE, *Southern Arabia*, London: Smith Elder & Co, 1908

BERQUE, JACQUES, *The Arabs: their History and Future*, London: Faber, 1964

BURCKHARDT, JOHN LEWIS, *Travels in Arabia*, London: Colburn, 1829

BURY, GEORGE W., *Arabia Infelix*, London: Macmillan, 1915

CHARLESWORTH, MARTIN P., *Trade Routes and Commerce of the Roman Empire*, Cambridge: University Press, 1924

FRANKFORT, HENRI, *The Birth of Civilization in the Near East*, London: Williams & Norgate, 1951

GLUEK, NELSON, *Deities and Dolphins*, London: Cassell, 1966

HALEVY, JOSEPH, *Rapport sur une mission archéologique dans le Yémen*, Paris: Imprimerie Nationale, 1872

HOGARTH, DAVID G., *The Penetration of Arabia*, London: Lawrence & Bullen, 1904

INGRAMS, W. H., *The Yemen*, London: Murray, 1963

ISIDORE OF CHARAX, *Parthian Stations*, translated by W. H. Schoff, Philadelphia: Commercial Museum, 1914

MILLER, JAMES I., *The Spice Trade of the Roman Empire*, Oxford: Clarendon Press, 1969

Periplus of the Erythraean Sea, translated by J. W. McCrindle, Calcutta: Thacker, Spink & Co, 1879

PHILBY, H. ST JOHN, *The Land of Midian*, London: Benn, 1957

PHILLIPS, WENDELL, *Qataban and Sheba*, London: Gollancz, 1955

POLANYI, KARL, *Trade and Markets in the Early Empires*, Glencoe, Ill: Free Press, 1957

ROTHENBURG, BENO, *God's Wilderness*, Thames & Hudson, 1961

SCOTT, HUGH, *In the High Yemen*, London: Murray, 1947

THESIGER, WILFRED PATRICK, *Arabian Sands*, London: Longman, 1959

THOMAS, BERTRAM SIDNEY, *Arabia Felix. Across the Empty Quarter*, London: Cape, 1932

TOY, BARBARA, *The Highway of the Three Kings*, London: Murray, 1968

VINCENT, WILLIAM, *The Commerce and Navigation of the Ancients in the Indian Ocean*, London: printed for T. Cadell and W. Davies, 1807

WARMINGTON, E. H., *The Commerce between the Roman Empire and India*, Cambridge: University Press, 1928

WELLSTED, JAMES RAYMOND, *Travels in Arabia*, London: Murray, 1838

WINDER, RICHARD B., *South Arabia in the Nineteenth Century*, London: Macmillan, 1965

The Silk Road

BOULNOIS, LUCE, *La Route de la Soie*, Paris: Gallimard, 1964

CHARLESWORTH, M. P., *Trade Routes and Commerce of the Roman Empire*, London: Oxford University Press, 1926

CORDIER, HENRI, *Ser Marco Polo*, London: Murray, 1920

FA-HSIEN, *The Travels*, translated by H. A. Giles, Cambridge: University Press, 1923

FERRIER, J. P., *Caravan Journeys and Wanderings in Persia, Afghanistan, and Turkestan*, London: Murray, 1856

FLEMING, ROBERT PETER, *News from Tartary*, London: Cape, 1936

HEDIN, SVEN ANDERS, *Across the Gobi Desert*, London: Routledge, 1931

—, *The Silk Road*, London: Routledge, 1938

HIRTH, FRIEDRICH, *China and the Roman Orient*, Leipsic and Munich: G. Hirth, 1885

HUDSON, G. F., *Europe and China: a Survey of their Relations from the earliest times to 1800*, London: E. Arnold & Co, 1931

LATTIMORE, OWEN, *The Desert Road to Turkestan*, London: Methuen, 1929

MAILLART, ELLA, *Forbidden Journey. From Peking to Kashmir*, London: Heinemann, 1937

POLO, MARCO, *The Travels*, edited by Manuel Komroff, Rochester, N.Y., Leo Hart, 1933

RUBRUQUIS, GULIELMUS DE, *Travels: the Journey of William Rubrick*, London: The Hakluyt Society, 1900

SELIGMAN, C. G., 'The Roman Orient and the Far East', *Antiquity*, 1937

STEIN, SIR MARC AUREL, 'Central Asian Relics of China's Ancient Silk Trade', Friedrich Hirth Anniversary Volume, 1923

—, *On Ancient Central-Asian Tracks*, London: Macmillan, 1933

—, *Ruins of Desert Cathay*, London: Macmillan, 1912

TEGGART, F., *Rome and China*, Berkeley, Calif: University Press, 1939

TEICHMAN, SIR ERIC, *Journey to Turkestan*, London: Hodder & Stoughton, 1937

VAMBERY, ARMINIUS (Armin Vamberg), *Travels in Central Asia*, London: Murray, 1864

YULE, SIR HENRY, *Cathay and the Way Thither*, Hakluyt Society, 1866

The Gold, Salt, and Slave Roads

BLAKE, WILLIAM O., *History of Slavery and the Slave Trade*, Columbus, Ohio: H. Miller, 1860

BOAHEN, ALBERT A., *Britain, the Sahara, and the Western Sudan, 1768–1861*, Oxford: Clarendon Press, 1964

BONNEL DE MEZIERES, ALBERT, *Le Major Laing*, Paris: Imprimerie Nationale, 1912

BOUREL DE LA RONCIERE, CHARLES GERMAIN, *La Decouverte de l'Afrique au Moyen Age*, Cairo: Memoires de la Société Royale de Géographie d'Egypte, Tome 5, 6, 1924–25

BOVILL, E. W., *Caravans of the Old Sahara*, London: Oxford University Press, 1970

BROSSET, CAPTAIN D., 'La Saline d'Idjil', *Bulletin du Comité de l'Afrique Française*, No 11 (1933)

BURCKHARDT, JOHN LEWIS, *Travels in Egypt and Nubia*, London: Murray, 1822

CAILLIE, RENE, *Travels through Central Africa to Timbuctoo, 1824–28*, London: Colburn & Bentley, 1830

CAPOT-REY, ROBERT, *Le Sahara Français*. Paris: Presses Universitaires, 1949

CHUDEAU, R., *Sahara Soudanais*, Paris: Colin, 1908

CORTIER, LIEUTENANT, 'De Tombouctou à Taodeni', *La Géographie*, XIV (1906)

DAUMAS, GENERAL EUGENE and M. AUSONE DE CHANCEL, *La Grand Desert, ou itinéraire d'une caravane au pays des nègres*, Paris: Chaix, 1848

DENHAM, DIXON and others, *Narrative of Travels and Discoveries . . . in 1822, 1823, and 1824*, London: Murray, 1826

DUBOIS, FELIX, *Timbuctoo the Mysterious*, London: Heinemann, 1896

FISHER, A. B., and H. J., *Slavery and Muslim Society in Africa*, London: Hurst, 1970

GRANDIN, CAPTAIN, 'KAWAR', *Bulletin de l'Institut de l'Afrique Noire*, XIII (1951)

HORNEMANN, FRIEDRICH CONRAD, *The Journal of Travels from Cairo to Mourzouk*, London: G. & W. Nichol, 1802

INGRAM, J. K., *History of Slavery and Serfdom*, London: Black, 1895

JACKSON, JAMES GREY, *An Account of Timbuctoo*, London: Cass Library of African Studies, No 25, 1912

LAING, MAJOR ALEXANDER GORDON, The Letters, 1824–26, *Missions to the Niger*, Vol I, The Hakluyt Society, 1964

LEO AFRICANUS, *The History and Description of Africa . . . done into English in 1600 by J. Pory and now edited by Dr. Robert Brown*, The Hakluyt Society, 1896

LHOTE, HENRI, *L'Epopée du Ténéré*, Paris: Gallimard, 1961

LYON, GEORGE F., *A Narrative of Travels in North Africa*, London: Murray, 1821

MINER, HORACE, *The Primitive City of Timbuctoo*, Princeton: University Press, 1961

NIEGER, MARIE JOSEPH EMILE, 'Mission du Transafricain', *La Géographie*, XVI (1907)

PELLOW, THOMAS, *The Adventures of Thos Pellow, Mariner*, edited by Dr Robert Brown, London: Unwin, 1890

PRUD'HOMME, CAPTAIN, 'Le Sebkha d'Idjil', *Bulletin Comité Historique et Scientifique de l'Afrique Français*, V (1925)

RAFFENEL, ANNE, *Nouveau Voyage dans le Pays des Nègres*, Paris: Bertrand, 1846

RICHARDSON, JAMES, *Narrative of a Mission to Central Africa*, London: Murray, 1853

RILEY, JAMES, *Sufferings in Africa. The Authentic Narrative of the Loss of the American Brig Commerce*, New York: Potter, 1965

SKOLLE, J., *The Road to Timbuktu*, London: Gollancz 1956

TRIMINGHAM, JOHN SPENCER, *A History of Islam in West Africa*, London: Oxford University Press, 1970

VISCHER, HANNS, *Across the Sahara from Tripoli to Bornu*, London: Arnold 1910

WELLARD, JAMES, *Lost Worlds of Africa*, London: Hutchinson, 1966

—, *The Great Sahara*, London: Hutchinson, 1964

Pilgrims' Caravans

BARTHEMA, LODOVICO, *The Itinerary . . . 1502–8*, London: Argonaut Press, 1928

BURTON, SIR RICHARD, *Personal Narrative of a Pilgrimage to Al-Madinah and Meccah*, London: Longmans, 1855

GAUDEFROY-DEMOMBYNES, MAURICE, *Le Pélérinage à Mecca*, Paris: l'Annales du Musée Guimel. Bibliographie d'Etudes, Tome 33 (1923)

HUGHES, THOMAS PATRICK, *Notes on Muhammedanism*, London: Allen, 1877

KEANE, JOHN F., *Six Months in Meccah*, London: Tinsley Bros, 1881

PITTS, JOSEPH, *A Faithful Account of the Religion and Manners of the Mahometans*, London: Osborne and Longman, 1731

SILVIA AQUITANIA, *The Pilgrimage of S. Silvia to the Places, circa 385 A.D*, London: Palestine Pilgrims Text Society, vol 1 (1891)

Military Caravans

ALFORD, H. S. L., *The Egyptian Sudan: its Loss and Recovery*, London: Macmillan, 1898

BREMOND, GENERAL EDOUARD, *Le Hedjaz dans la Guerre Mondiale*, Paris: Gautier Villars, 1931

BOVILL, E. H., 'Camels in Roman Africa', *Antiquity*, 1956

BROGAN, OLIVE, 'Camels in Tripolitania', Papers of the British School of Rome, 1954

CARBUCCIA, GENERAL J. L. S. B., *Du Dromedaire comme Bête de Somme et comme Animal de Guerre*, Paris: Dumaire, 1853

COLBOURNE, J., *With Hicks Pasha in the Sudan*, London: Smith, Elder, 1884

DEBEVOISE, N. C., *Political History of Parthia*, Chicago: University Press, 1938

FELTON, C. C., *Life of William Eaton*, Library of American Biography, vol 9, 1838

GERMAIN, JOSE, *Le Général Laperrine*, Paris: Editions Medicis, 1931

LAWRENCE, T. E., *Seven Pillars of Wisdom*, Penguin Modern Classics, no. 1696 (1962)

LEPPER, FRANCIS A., *Trajan's Parthian War*, London: Oxford University Press, 1948

LESQUIER, JEAN, *L'Armée Romaine d'Egypte*, Cairo: Memoires de l'Institut, Tome 41 (1918)

PAOLO DELLA CELLA, *Narrative of an Expedition from Tripoli in Barbary to the Western Frontier of Egypt*, London: Murray, 1822

ROSTOVTZEFF, M., *The Social and Economic History of the Roman Empire*, London: Oxford University Press, 1926

WEBSTER, GRAHAM, *The Roman Imperial Army*, London: Black, 1969

America

CARROLL, CHARLES S., 'The Government's Importation of Camels: a Historical Sketch', U.S. Dept of Agriculture, Bureau of Animal Industry, Circular No 53 (1904)

FALK, ODIE B., *The U.S. Camel Corps, An Army Experiment*, New York: Oxford University Press, 1976

FOWLER, HARLAN D., *Camels to California*, Stanford, Calif.: University Press, 1950

GRAY, A. A., FARQUAR, F. P., and WILLIAM LEWIS. *Camels in Western America*, San Francisco: California Historical Society, 1930

GUINN, J. M., 'Camel Caravans of the American Deserts', Historical Society of Southern California Annual Publications, V, Part II, No III (1901)

HALL, S. M., 'The Camels in the Southwest', *Out West*, XXVI (1907)

'Jeff Davis's Camel Experiment', *Popular Science Monthly*, LXXIV (1909)

LESLEY, LEWIS B., *Uncle Sam's Camels*, Cambridge: Harvard University Press, 1929

LEWIS, W. S., 'The Camel Pack Trains in the Mining Camps of the West', *Washington Historical Quarterly*, XIX No 4 (1928)

MARSH, GEORGE P., *The Camel: His Origin, Habits, and Uses Considered with Reference to His Introduction into the U.S.*, Boston: Harvard, 1856

Australia

BARKER, HERBERT M., *Camels and the Outback*, London: Angus & Robertson, 1964

CLUNE, FRANK, *Overland Telegraph*, Sydney: Angus & Robertson, 1955

FINLAYSON, HEDLEY H., *The Red Centre*, Sydney: Angus & Robertson, 1935

GILES, ERNEST, *Australia Twice Traversed*, London: Sampson, Low, 1889

GREY, SIR GEORGE, *Journals of Two Expeditions . . . in 1837 and 39*, London: Murray, 1847

HARCUS, WILLIAM, *History of South Australia*, Adelaide: W. C. Cox, 1876

MADIGAN, CECIL T., *Central Australia*, London: Oxford University Press, 1936

MCPHEAT, WILLIAM S., *John Flynn*, London: Hodder & Stoughton, 1963

MOOREHEAD, ALAN, *Cooper's Creek*, London: Hamish Hamilton, 1963

PLOWMAN, R. BRUCE, *Camel Pads*, Sydney: Angus & Robertson, 1933

—, *The Man from Oodnadatta*, Sydney: Angus & Robertson, 1933

SCOTT, G. FIRTH, *The Romance of Australian Exploring*, London: Sampson, Low, 1899

TERRY, MICHAEL, *Sand and Sun*, London: Michael Joseph, 1937

WARBURTON, PETER EGERTON, *Journey across the Western Interior of Australia*, London: Sampson, Low, 1875

Index